AF824200

Buy Your First Home: For Black Women

By Michaela Dosunmu

Disclaimer:

The information contained in this book is for educational and informational purposes only. It is not intended as a substitute for professional advice, whether medical, psychological, financial, or otherwise. The author is not a licensed healthcare or mental health professional. Readers should seek advice from their physician, therapist, or other qualified professionals for any personal concerns related to health, habits, or behavior change.

While the practices and techniques discussed in this book are based on research and the author's experiences, individual results may vary. The recommendations in this book should be considered complementary to conventional medical, psychological, or professional care, and not as a replacement.

The author and publisher disclaim any liability for any direct or indirect consequences arising from the use of the information in this book. It is essential to consult with a qualified professional before implementing any significant lifestyle or behavioral changes, especially if you have a medical condition or specific personal circumstances.

By reading this book, you acknowledge that the information is not intended to diagnose or treat any condition and is provided on an "as-is" basis.

Table Of Contents

Introduction

Buying your first home is one of the most exciting and important decisions you can make. It's not just about having a place to live; it's about having something that's truly yours. A home is where you can feel safe, create memories, and build a future. But for many people, the idea of buying a home can feel a little scary. There's a lot to learn, and it might seem like there are too many steps or things to think about. That's why this book was written—to make things simple and clear, so you can feel ready and confident to take this big step.

For Black women, buying a home carries even more meaning. It's not just about owning property; it's about breaking barriers and creating opportunities. Historically, many challenges have made homeownership difficult, from unfair lending practices to unequal opportunities. Despite these challenges, Black women have always shown strength and determination, pushing forward to build better lives for themselves and their families. This book celebrates that strength and offers guidance to help you achieve your dream of owning a home.

Owning a home is about more than money or having a roof over your head. It's about creating a space that reflects who you are. It's about feeling a sense of pride every time you step through the door. When you own a home, you're building stability—not just for yourself, but for your family and even future generations. A home can be a place of comfort, joy, and growth. It's where you can feel free to be yourself and where your dreams can grow.

If you're feeling unsure or overwhelmed about buying a home, that's okay. Many people feel that way at first. The process can seem complicated, with terms like mortgages, down payments, and credit scores. This book is here to make those things simple. Each chapter breaks down what you need to know step by step. Whether you're just starting to think about buying a home or already getting ready to make an offer, you'll find advice and tips to help you every step of the way.

One of the most important things to remember is that buying a home doesn't happen overnight. It takes planning, saving, and learning. But every small step you take brings you closer to your goal. This book will show you how to check your finances, find the right neighborhood, and choose a home that fits your needs. It will also teach you about the hidden costs of owning a home, like maintenance and repairs, so you'll be prepared for what comes next.

Homeownership is also a powerful way to build wealth. When you own a home, its value can grow over time. That means the longer you own it, the more it can be worth. This can help you create financial security for yourself and even for your family in the future. A home can be passed down to children or used to fund new opportunities, like starting a business or pursuing education. It's a way to create something lasting that benefits not just you, but also the people you care about.

This book also understands that buying a home as a Black woman can come with unique challenges. There may be moments when the process feels harder because of past or present barriers. But it's important to know that there are resources and programs designed to help you. You are not alone in this. The book includes practical advice for overcoming challenges and finding the support you need. It also shares stories of other Black women who have achieved their dreams of homeownership, showing you that it's possible for you too.

Once you've bought your home, the journey doesn't end there. Owning a home means taking care of it and making it your own. You'll learn how to keep up with maintenance, handle unexpected repairs, and stay on top of expenses. This book will also help you think about the future—whether that means saving for your next home, using your home to build more wealth, or simply enjoying the life you've worked so hard to create.

The purpose of this book is to empower you. It's written to give you the knowledge, confidence, and inspiration to take charge of your homeownership journey. No matter where you're starting from, you can achieve your dream of owning a home. By the time you finish reading, you'll have a clear plan and the tools you need to turn your dream into reality. Remember, buying a home is not just about the house itself—it's about creating a better future for yourself and the people you love.

1

Understanding the Importance of Homeownership

Why Homeownership Matters

Owning a home is one of the most important steps you can take in life. It's not just about having a place to live. Homeownership can give you financial security, emotional peace, and stronger connections with your community. Let's look at why owning a home is so valuable.

Financial Benefits of Owning a Home

One of the biggest reasons people want to own a home is to build financial security. When you rent, your monthly payments go to your landlord, and you don't get any lasting benefits. But when you own a home, your monthly mortgage payments help you buy something that's yours. Over time, you build something called equity. Equity is the portion of the house that you truly own, not the bank. The more you pay off your mortgage, the more equity you have.

Another important financial benefit is stability. When you rent, your landlord can raise the rent every year. This can make it hard to plan your money. But when you own a home with a fixed-rate mortgage, your monthly payments stay the same for years. This makes it easier to plan your budget and feel secure about your finances.

Homes can also increase in value over time. This is called appreciation. If your home becomes worth more than what you paid for it, you can sell it later and make a profit. That money can be used for other goals, like sending your children to college, starting a business, or saving for retirement.

Finally, owning a home can help you access credit in the future. If you need money for big expenses, like a medical emergency or repairs, you can borrow against the value of your home. This is called a home equity loan. While it's important to borrow wisely, this option can provide financial flexibility.

Emotional Benefits of Owning a Home

Owning a home brings a deep sense of pride. It's your space, and you can make it exactly how you like. You can paint the walls, hang up family pictures, and design every room to fit your style. This is different from renting, where you often need permission to make changes.

A home also brings a sense of security. When you rent, there's always a chance your landlord might sell the property or ask you to leave. But when you own your home, it's yours. You don't have to worry about unexpected changes or losing your living space. This feeling of stability is priceless, especially for families.

Your home can also be a place of comfort and peace. It's where you can relax after a long day, spend time with loved ones, and create special memories. It becomes more than just a building; it becomes part of your life story.

Social Benefits of Owning a Home

Owning a home can help you feel more connected to your community. Homeowners often take pride in their neighbourhoods. They get to know their neighbours, participate in local events, and work together to improve the area. These connections can make your community feel safer and more welcoming.

When you own a home, you're also more likely to stay in one place for a longer time. This stability allows you to build stronger relationships with the people around you. You might make friends with your neighbours, join local groups, or volunteer for community projects. These activities can improve not just your life but also the lives of others around you.

For Black women, owning a home is a powerful way to set an example for others. When you achieve homeownership, it shows that it's possible for others in your family or community to do the same. It inspires younger generations to work toward their own goals and believe in their ability to succeed.

Generational Wealth and Homeownership

One of the most lasting benefits of owning a home is the ability to create generational wealth. Generational wealth means passing down financial assets, like a house, to your children or other family members. This gives them a strong start in life and helps them avoid some of the financial struggles you may have faced.

For example, if you own your home, your children might inherit it someday. They won't have to worry about paying rent or buying a house from scratch. They can use the money saved on housing for education, investments, or other important goals.

Generational wealth also helps strengthen communities. When more families own homes, they can build financial security together. This creates stronger, healthier communities where everyone has a chance to thrive.

A Step Toward Independence

Homeownership is a step toward financial and personal independence. It allows you to take control of your living situation and your future. Instead of depending on a landlord or worrying about rent increases, you can make decisions based on what's best for you and your family.

For Black women, owning a home is also a way to reclaim control in a system that has often worked against them. Despite historical challenges in accessing fair housing opportunities, homeownership is a way to overcome these barriers and create a better future.

Overcoming Systemic Barriers

Black women have faced many challenges when trying to own a home. These challenges did not start today but are rooted in history. Understanding these barriers helps us see how they still affect the housing market today and what steps can be taken to overcome them.

The History of Discrimination in Housing

For a long time, Black people, including Black women, were not given the same opportunities as others to buy homes. In the past, there were laws and policies that made it harder for Black families to own property. One example is a practice called "redlining." This meant that banks and lenders marked certain neighbourhoods, mostly where Black people lived, as "high risk." Because of this, they refused to give loans to people who lived in these areas, even if they could afford to buy a home.

This discrimination was not only unfair but also stopped Black families from building wealth through homeownership. While other groups were buying homes and growing their financial security, Black families were left behind. This gap in wealth and opportunity has carried on through generations.

Unequal Access to Fair Lending

Even after laws were passed to stop housing discrimination, Black women continued to face unfair treatment. Many were given loans with higher interest rates than others, even when they had the same financial qualifications. This is called "predatory lending." These loans often cost more over time and made it harder for Black women to keep their homes or pay off their mortgages.

Another challenge is that Black women often earn less money than others, even when they are doing the same job. For example, studies show that Black women in the United States make about 63 cents for every dollar that white men earn. This wage gap makes it harder to save money for things like a down payment, monthly payments, or even qualifying for loans. Even though they work hard, many Black women face these struggles simply because of who they are.

Limited Representation in Real Estate

Limited Representation in Real Estate

The real estate industry has not always welcomed or supported Black women. In the past, some real estate agents refused to show homes in certain neighborhoods to Black buyers. This practice, called "racial steering," stopped Black families from moving to areas with better schools, jobs, and resources. For example, during the mid-20th century, Black families in cities like Chicago and Detroit were often denied access to suburban neighborhoods due to real estate practices and agreements that only allowed white families to live there. Another example is Levittown, New York, a suburban community built after World War II, where Black families were deliberately excluded from buying homes. These actions kept Black families from building wealth and accessing better opportunities for their children.

Even today, Black women may find it harder to connect with real estate professionals who understand their needs or respect their goals. Representation matters, and having professionals who advocate for fair treatment can make a big difference in the home-buying process.

How These Challenges Shape Today's Housing Market

The struggles Black women have faced in the past continue to affect their chances of owning homes today. The wealth gap created by years of discrimination means many Black women start with fewer resources than others. High housing costs, unequal lending practices, and limited access to financial education make the process even harder.

However, progress is being made. There are now laws and programs designed to support Black women and other minorities in becoming homeowners. For example, organizations like the National Association of Real Estate Brokers (NAREB) run initiatives such as the "Two Million New Black Homeowners" program, which aims to increase Black homeownership through education, advocacy, and access to resources. Additionally, first-time buyer programs like Down Payment Assistance Programs **(DAPs)** help reduce the upfront costs of buying a home, making it more affordable for Black women to achieve their dreams of homeownership.

Moving Forward

Overcoming systemic barriers requires persistence and support. It means understanding the challenges, knowing your rights, and seeking resources that can help. Black women have shown incredible strength and resilience in the face of these obstacles. By continuing to push for fairness and equality in the housing market, they are shaping a better future for themselves and future generations.

Homeownership is a path to independence and security, and Black women deserve the same opportunities as anyone else. While the road has been hard, every step forward brings us closer to a world where everyone can achieve their dreams of owning a home.

The Power of Homeownership

Owning a home is more than just having a place to live. For Black women, homeownership is a powerful tool to build financial independence and generational wealth. It provides stability, opens doors to financial growth, and helps secure a better future for families. Let's explore how owning a home can create long-term benefits.

Building Generational Wealth

Generational wealth means passing something valuable to your children or other family members. For many people, a home is one of the most important things they can leave behind. When you own a home, its value can grow over time. This growth in value is called appreciation. If you decide to sell the house later, you might earn more than you paid for it. This extra money can be passed down to your children, helping them start their lives with financial support.

For example, a home can provide a stable living space for generations. If you leave your home to your children, they won't need to worry about paying rent or buying their own house right away. They can use the money they save on housing for education, starting a business, or investing in their future. This cycle helps families grow stronger financially over time.

Financial Independence

Homeownership gives Black women a sense of control over their finances. Unlike renting, where monthly payments go to a landlord, mortgage payments go toward something you own. As you pay off your mortgage, you build equity. Equity is the part of the home that belongs to you, not the bank. This is like having money saved up in your property.

Having equity also gives you options. You can use it to take out loans for important expenses, like starting a business or paying for college. These loans, called home equity loans, often have lower interest rates than other types of loans. This makes them a better option for borrowing money when needed.

Owning a home also helps protect you from rising rent costs. Rent can go up every year, making it harder to budget. But when you have a fixed-rate mortgage, your monthly payments stay the same. This stability allows you to plan your expenses and feel secure about your finances.

Stability and Pride

Owning a home is about more than just money—it's about having a stable place to call your own. A home gives you freedom to make decisions that fit your life. You can decorate, renovate, and create a space that reflects your personality and values. This sense of ownership brings pride and confidence, especially for Black women who have faced challenges in the housing market.

A stable home also provides a foundation for raising a family. Children grow up in a secure environment, with fewer disruptions like moving due to rent increases or landlord decisions. This stability helps families focus on other goals, like education and career growth.

Breaking Cycles of Inequality

For many Black women, owning a home is a way to overcome historical and systemic barriers. Discrimination in housing has kept many Black families from building wealth in the past. By becoming homeowners, Black women are breaking these cycles and creating new opportunities for their families.

Homeownership also helps strengthen communities. When Black women own homes, they invest in their neighbourhoods. They become role models, showing others that financial independence and success are possible.

A Step Toward the Future

The power of homeownership lies in the opportunities it creates. It's not just about owning property—it's about building a foundation for financial growth, stability, and independence. For Black women, owning a home is a step toward a brighter future, where they can achieve their goals and leave a lasting legacy for their families.

2

Preparing Yourself Financially

Assessing Your Financial Health

Before you buy a home, it's important to understand where you stand financially. This means taking a close look at your credit score, income, and debt-to-income ratio. Knowing these things will help you see if you're ready to buy a house or if you need to make some changes first. Let's break it down step by step.

What is a Credit Score and Why Does It Matter?

A credit score is a number that shows how well you've managed money you've borrowed in the past. It's like a report card for your finances. Lenders, like banks, look at your credit score to decide if they can trust you to pay back a loan. The higher your score, the better.

If you have a good credit score, you're more likely to get approved for a mortgage. You'll also get better interest rates, which means paying less money over time. A low credit score might make it harder to get a loan, or you might get one with higher interest, which costs more.

You can check your credit score by using free tools online or by requesting a credit report from credit bureaus. Look at your report to make sure everything is correct. If there are mistakes, you can ask to have them fixed. If your credit score isn't where you want it to be, don't worry. You can improve it by paying bills on time, reducing debt, and avoiding new credit cards before applying for a mortgage.

Major Credit Bureaus in the U.S.

Here are the three main credit bureaus in the U.S. where you can request your credit report:

1. Equifax
   - Website: www.equifax.com
   - Phone: 1-800-685-1111
2. Experian
   - Website: www.experian.com
   - Phone: 1-888-397-3742
3. TransUnion
   - Website: www.transunion.com
   - Phone: 1-800-916-8800

You're entitled to one free credit report per year from each of these bureaus through AnnualCreditReport.com or by calling 1-877-322-8228.

Checking Your Income Stability

When you apply for a mortgage, lenders want to see that you have a steady income. They'll check how much money you make each month and whether your job is stable. This shows them that you'll be able to make your monthly payments without any trouble.

If your income is not consistent, for example, if you work freelance or have multiple jobs, you might need to show extra proof. This can include bank statements, tax returns, or contracts. The goal is to show that you can afford to pay your mortgage every month.

Take a moment to look at your income. Write down how much money you bring in each month. Make sure to include all sources, like your main job, side gigs, or any other earnings. Then, compare this to your regular expenses to see how much money you have left over. This leftover money is what you could use for a mortgage.

Understanding Your Debt-to-Income Ratio

Your debt-to-income ratio (DTI) is another thing lender will check. It's a number that shows how much of your monthly income goes toward paying debts. This includes things like credit card payments, car loans, student loans, and any other debts.

To calculate your DTI, add up all your monthly debt payments. Then, divide that number by your monthly income and multiply by 100 to get a percentage. For example, if you earn $4,000 a month and spend $1,200 on debt, your DTI is 30%.

Most lenders in the USA prefer a DTI of 43% or lower. If your DTI is higher, it might mean you're carrying too much debt, and lenders could see you as a higher risk. In that case, focus on paying off some debts before applying for a mortgage.

Why Assessing Your Financial Health is Important?

Taking the time to understand your credit score, income stability, and DTI ratio helps you see the big picture of your financial health. It shows you what you can afford and helps you avoid surprises during the home-buying process. If something doesn't look right, like a low credit score or too much debt, you can work on improving it.

By getting your finances in order now, you're setting yourself up for success. You'll be more confident when talking to lenders, and you'll have a better chance of getting the home you want at a price you can manage. Preparing financially is the first step toward turning your dream of homeownership into a reality.

Creating a Home-Buying Budget

Buying a home is a big financial step, and having a good budget is the key to making it work. A home-buying budget helps you save for the three main things you'll need: a down payment, closing costs, and emergency funds. Let's go over how you can plan for each of these.

Saving for a Down Payment

The down payment is the amount of money you pay upfront when buying a home. It's a percentage of the home's price, and the rest is covered by your mortgage. Most lenders ask for a down payment of at least 3% to 20% of the home's price, depending on the type of loan you choose.

For example, if you're looking at a home that costs $200,000 and the lender requires a 10% down payment, you'll need $20,000. If you can save more than the minimum down payment, it's even better. A larger down payment lowers the amount you borrow, which means smaller monthly payments and less interest over time.

Start by figuring out how much you can set aside each month for your down payment. Cut back on unnecessary expenses and put that money into a savings account. You can also look into programs that help first-time buyers with down payments or grants specifically for Black women and minority homebuyers.

Planning for Closing Costs

Closing costs are the fees you pay when you officially buy the home. These can include things like loan origination fees, title insurance, home inspections, and appraisals. Closing costs are usually about 2% to 5% of the home's price.

Using the same $200,000 home example, you might need an additional $4,000 to $10,000 for closing costs. Make sure to include these expenses in your budget so you're not caught off guard.

You can ask your lender for an estimate of closing costs when you get pre-approved for a mortgage. This will help you plan better. Some buyers negotiate with sellers to cover part of these costs, but it's always good to be prepared to pay them yourself.

Setting Aside Emergency Funds

After buying a home, unexpected expenses can come up. You might need to fix a leaky roof, replace a broken water heater, or handle other repairs. That's why it's important to have an emergency fund ready.

Experts recommend saving three to six months' worth of living expenses in an emergency fund. This money is separate from your down payment and closing costs. It's there to give you peace of mind in case something goes wrong after you move in.

If saving for an emergency fund feels overwhelming, start small. Even setting aside $50 or $100 a month can add up over time. The important thing is to be consistent.

Building Credit and Reducing Debt

Before applying for a mortgage, it's important to have a good credit score and manageable debt. Lenders look at your credit and debt to decide if you qualify for a loan and what kind of terms they can offer. Improving your credit and reducing debt might seem challenging, but it's possible with the right steps. Let's break it down into simple actions you can take.

What is a Credit Score?

Your credit score is a number that shows how trustworthy you are when it comes to borrowing money. It's based on things like how often you pay bills on time, how much debt you owe, and how long you've had credit. A good credit score makes it easier to get approved for a mortgage and can lower the interest rate on your loan.

Steps to Improve Your Credit Score

Pay Bills on Time

Paying your bills on time is one of the most important things you can do for your credit score. Late payments can lower your score and make lenders think you're not reliable. Set reminders or use automatic payments to make sure you don't miss any due dates.

Keep Credit Card Balances Low

The amount of money you owe on your credit cards compared to your credit limit is called your "credit utilization ratio." For example, if your credit limit is $1,000 and you owe $300, your ratio is 30%. Lenders prefer a ratio of 30% or lower. Try to pay down your balances to keep this ratio low.

Check Your Credit Report

Mistakes on your credit report can hurt your score. Check your report for errors, like accounts you don't recognize or payments that were marked late but were actually on time. You can request free reports from credit bureaus and dispute any errors you find.

Avoid Opening New Credit Accounts

Each time you apply for new credit, it creates a "hard inquiry" on your report, which can temporarily lower your score. Avoid opening new credit cards or taking on new loans while preparing for a mortgage.

Keep Old Accounts Open

The longer you've had credit, the better it looks to lenders. Even if you don't use an old credit card often, keeping it open can help your score. Just make sure there's no annual fee for keeping the account.

Why Reducing Debt is Important

Reducing debt shows lenders that you can manage your money well and that you'll be able to handle a mortgage. Too much debt can make it hard to qualify for a loan or leave you with a high-interest rate. Reducing your debt gives you more room in your budget for your mortgage payments and other expenses.

Steps to Reduce Debt

Create a Debt Payoff Plan

Write down all your debts, including credit cards, personal loans, and car loans. List how much you owe, the interest rate for each debt, and the minimum monthly payment. Start paying off the debt with the highest interest rate first, as it costs you the most over time. This is called the "avalanche method."

Alternatively, you can use the "snowball method" by paying off the smallest debt first. This helps build momentum and keeps you motivated.

Stop Using Credit Cards

If you're trying to reduce debt, avoid adding more to it. Use cash or a debit card for everyday expenses so you're not increasing your balances while trying to pay them down.

Cut Back on Unnecessary Spending

Look at your monthly expenses and see where you can save. Cancel subscriptions you don't use, eat out less, or switch to more affordable services. Use the extra money to pay off your debts faster.

Negotiate with Creditors

Sometimes, creditors are willing to lower your interest rates or monthly payments. Call your credit card company and ask if they can offer you a better rate or more manageable terms.

Consider a Debt Consolidation Loan

If you have multiple high-interest debts, you can combine them into one loan with a lower interest rate. This simplifies your payments and can save you money in the long run. Be cautious, though, and make sure the new loan's terms are better than what you currently have.

Staying on Track

Improving your credit score and reducing debt takes time, but it's worth the effort. Track your progress regularly and celebrate small wins, like paying off a credit card or raising your score by a few points. The better your financial health, the more confident you'll feel when applying for a mortgage.

Remember, building good credit and lowering debt not only helps you buy a home but also sets you up for long-term financial success. Start with small steps, stay consistent, and you'll be ready to take the next step toward homeownership.

Understanding the Costs of Homeownership

Owning a home is exciting, but it's also a big responsibility. Many people think the only cost of owning a home is the mortgage, but there are other expenses to plan for. These include utilities, maintenance, property taxes, and unexpected repairs. Let's look at these costs so you can be prepared.

Utilities

Utilities are the basic services that keep your home running. These include electricity, water, gas, and sometimes garbage collection. When you rent, some of these costs might be included in your rent, but as a homeowner, you'll need to pay them separately.

The cost of utilities depends on the size of your home, how many people live there, and your location. For example, larger homes usually use more electricity for heating or cooling. To save money, you can turn off lights when not in use, fix leaks, and choose energy-efficient appliances. Being careful with your usage can make a big difference in your monthly bills.

Maintenance

Every home need regular maintenance to keep it in good shape. This includes simple things like mowing the lawn, cleaning gutters, and replacing air filters. It also includes larger tasks, like painting the house or fixing small cracks before they become big problems.

Experts suggest setting aside about 1% of your home's value each year for maintenance. For example, if your home is worth $200,000, you should save $2,000 each year for maintenance. This helps you stay ready for regular upkeep and avoid big surprises later.

Property Taxes

When you own a home, you'll need to pay property taxes every year. These taxes are based on the value of your home and are used to fund things like schools, roads, and local services. The amount you owe depends on where you live, as different cities and states have different tax rates.

Property taxes are usually paid once a year, but some lenders include them in your monthly mortgage payment. They set up an escrow account where you pay a little extra each month, and the lender pays the taxes for you when they're due. Make sure you know how property taxes work in your area so you can plan for them.

Unexpected Repairs

No matter how well you maintain your home, unexpected repairs will happen. These can include things like a broken water heater, a leaking roof, or a burst pipe. Some repairs are small and affordable, but others can cost thousands of dollars.

To handle these surprises, it's important to have an emergency fund. This is money you set aside just for repairs. Experts recommend saving three to six months of living expenses for emergencies. If that feels like too much, start small and add to it over time. Even having $500 to $1,000 saved can help with smaller repairs.

You can also consider a home warranty. This is a service plan that covers the cost of repairing or replacing major systems, like your HVAC or appliances, for a yearly fee. While it doesn't cover everything, it can help reduce the financial burden of some repairs.

Other Costs to Consider

There are a few other costs you should be aware of as a homeowner:

Insurance

Homeowners insurance is required by most lenders and protects your home from damage caused by events like fires, storms, or theft. Be sure to shop around for the best rates and coverage.

HOA Fees

If you live in a neighbourhood with a homeowner's association (HOA), you'll need to pay monthly or yearly fees. These fees are used to maintain common areas, like parks or pools.

Landscaping

If your home has a yard, you may need to budget for things like lawn care, tree trimming, or gardening supplies.

Planning for the Costs

The best way to handle the costs of homeownership is to plan ahead. Make a list of all the possible expenses and set up a budget that includes them. This way, you won't be caught off guard when a bill arrives or a repair is needed.

Homeownership is a wonderful achievement, but it's important to understand the full picture. By planning for utilities, maintenance, taxes, and unexpected repairs, you can enjoy your home without unnecessary stress. Being prepared makes all the difference.

3

Understanding Mortgage Basics

Buying a home is one of the biggest financial decisions you'll ever make, and understanding how mortgages work is an important step. A mortgage is a loan that helps you pay for a home. Since most people don't have the full amount of money to buy a house upfront, they borrow from a bank or lender and pay it back over time. Let's explore the basics of mortgages, starting with the different types and what you need to qualify.

Types of Mortgages

There are several types of mortgages to choose from. Each type has its own rules and benefits, so it's important to find the one that fits your needs. Here's an overview of the main options:

Fixed-Rate Mortgages

- A fixed-rate mortgage has the same interest rate for the entire life of the loan. This means your monthly payment will stay the same, making it easier to plan your budget.
- These loans are usually available in terms of 15, 20, or 30 years. A shorter loan term means higher monthly payments but less interest paid overall. A longer term means lower monthly payments but more interest over time.
- Fixed-rate mortgages are a good choice if you plan to stay in your home for a long time or prefer stable, predictable payments.

Adjustable-Rate Mortgages (ARMs)

- With an adjustable-rate mortgage, the interest rate starts low for a set period, such as 5, 7, or 10 years. After that, the rate can change yearly based on market conditions.

- The initial lower rate can make ARMs appealing, but your monthly payment may go up or down later, depending on how the rate changes.
- ARMs can be a good choice if you plan to sell or refinance before the initial fixed period ends.

FHA Loans

- FHA loans are backed by the Federal Housing Administration and are designed for people with lower credit scores or smaller down payments.
- They require a down payment as low as 3.5% and have more flexible credit requirements than conventional loans.
- These loans are great for first-time homebuyers or those who might not qualify for other types of loans. However, FHA loans require mortgage insurance, which adds to your monthly costs.

VA Loans

- VA loans are for active-duty military members, veterans, and their families. These loans are backed by the Department of Veterans Affairs and often require no down payment.
- They don't require private mortgage insurance (PMI), which can save you money, and usually have lower interest rates than conventional loans.
- VA loans are a great option for those who qualify, offering affordable terms and benefits.

USDA Loans

- USDA loans are backed by the U.S. Department of Agriculture and are designed for people buying homes in rural or suburban areas.
- These loans often require no down payment and offer low-interest rates, but they do have income limits and location requirements.

- If you're buying a home in an eligible area and meet the income criteria, USDA loans can be an excellent choice.

Conventional Loans

- Conventional loans are not backed by the government. They usually require a higher credit score and a larger down payment, often at least 5%.
- These loans come in fixed-rate and adjustable-rate options. They also don't require mortgage insurance if you put down at least 20%.
- Conventional loans are ideal for buyers with strong credit and enough savings for a larger down payment.

Determining Your Mortgage Eligibility

Before you can get a mortgage, lenders will look at several factors to decide if you qualify and how much you can borrow. These factors help them determine how risky it is to lend you money. Let's break down the key thing's lenders consider.

Income

- Lenders need to know you have enough money to pay back the loan. They'll ask for proof of income, such as pay stubs, tax returns, or bank statements.
- Your income helps them calculate how much you can afford for monthly mortgage payments. If you have steady, reliable income, you're more likely to qualify.

Debt-to-Income Ratio (DTI)

- Your debt-to-income ratio shows how much of your income goes toward paying debts. To calculate it, lenders divide your monthly debt payments by your gross monthly income.
- For example, if you earn $4,000 a month and pay $1,200 in debts, your DTI is 30%.

- Most lenders prefer a DTI of 43% or lower. A lower DTI shows you have enough income left to cover a mortgage payment.

Credit Score

- Your credit score is a key factor in getting approved for a mortgage. It's a number that reflects how well you've managed borrowing and repaying money in the past.
- A higher credit score makes you a lower-risk borrower, which can help you get a lower interest rate. Most lenders look for a score of at least 620 for conventional loans, but FHA loans may accept lower scores.
- To improve your credit score, pay bills on time, reduce debt, and avoid applying for new credit before getting a mortgage.

Employment History

- Lenders want to see that you have stable employment. This shows them you're likely to keep earning money to make your payments.
- They usually look for at least two years of consistent work in the same field. If you've recently changed jobs, you may need to explain how it fits your career path or show additional proof of income.

Down Payment

- The amount of money you can put down on the home affects your eligibility. A larger down payment reduces the amount you need to borrow and can make you a more attractive candidate to lenders.
- Some loans, like VA or USDA loans, require no down payment, but for others, the more you can save, the better your terms may be.

Savings and Assets

- Lenders may also look at your savings and other assets, like investments or retirement accounts. This helps them see if you have money set aside for emergencies or to cover your mortgage payments if something unexpected happens.

Loan Type and Amount

- The type of mortgage you apply for and the amount you want to borrow can also affect your eligibility. Different loans have different requirements, and lenders will check to see if your finances fit the guidelines.

Preparing to Apply for a Mortgage

To improve your chances of getting approved, start by reviewing your finances. Check your credit score, calculate your DTI, and gather proof of income and savings. If you notice any areas that need improvement, like high debt or low credit, work on fixing those before applying.

How to Choose the Right Loan for You

Choosing the right loan is one of the most important steps in buying a home. A good loan should fit your financial situation and make it easier to manage your payments. To find the best option, you need to compare loan types and understand how interest rates, terms, and conditions affect your choice. Let's break it down into simple steps.

Understand the Different Loan Types

There are several types of home loans, and each one works differently. Here's a quick look at the most common options:

Fixed-Rate Mortgages

- With this loan, the interest rate stays the same for the entire loan term. Your monthly payment will not change, making it easy to plan your budget.
- Fixed-rate loans usually come in 15-, 20-, or 30-year terms. A 30-year loan has lower monthly payments, while a 15-year loan helps you pay off your home faster but with higher payments.

Adjustable-Rate Mortgages (ARMs)

- This type of loan starts with a lower interest rate for a set period, such as 5 or 7 years. After that, the rate can change yearly based on market conditions.
- ARMs are good if you plan to sell or refinance before the rate adjusts. However, the changing rate can make your monthly payment unpredictable.

FHA Loans

- These loans are backed by the Federal Housing Administration and are great for first-time buyers. They allow for lower credit scores and smaller down payments, sometimes as low as 3.5%.
- FHA loans require mortgage insurance, which adds to your monthly costs, but they're a good choice if you're just starting out.

VA Loans

- VA loans are for veterans, active-duty military members, and their families. They usually require no down payment and don't have private mortgage insurance (PMI).
- These loans often come with lower interest rates and are an excellent option for those who qualify.

USDA Loans

- These loans are for people buying homes in rural or suburban areas. They often require no down payment and have low-interest rates.
- You must meet income and location requirements to qualify for a USDA loan.

Compare Interest Rates

The interest rate is the percentage you pay on top of the loan amount. Even a small difference in rates can make a big impact on your monthly payment and the total amount you pay over time.

- Fixed Rates: These rates stay the same for the life of the loan, offering stability.
- Variable Rates: These can go up or down, which may lower your initial payments but make them unpredictable later.

When comparing rates, look for the APR (Annual Percentage Rate). This includes the interest rate plus any fees, giving you a clearer picture of the loan's total cost.

Understand Loan Terms

The loan term is how long you have to repay the loan. Common terms are 15, 20, and 30 years. Here's how they differ:

Shorter Terms (15 or 20 years)

- Higher monthly payments.
- Less interest paid over time.
- You own your home faster.

Longer Terms (30 years)

- Lower monthly payments.
- More interest paid over time.
- Easier to manage in your monthly budget.

Choose a term that matches your financial comfort level. If you can afford higher payments, a shorter term will save you money in the long run.

Look at Loan Conditions

Loan conditions include the specific rules and requirements that come with your loan. These might include:

Down Payment Requirements

Some loans require higher down payments, while others, like VA or USDA loans, may require none.

Mortgage Insurance

Certain loans, like FHA or conventional loans with less than 20% down, require mortgage insurance. This adds to your monthly cost.

Prepayment Penalties

Some loans charge a fee if you pay off the loan early. Check to make sure your loan doesn't include this penalty if you plan to pay it off faster.

Closing Costs

These are fees you pay to finalize the loan, like appraisal fees or title insurance. Some lenders may offer to cover part of these costs, but it could mean a higher interest rate.

Match the Loan to Your Situation

To find the best loan, think about your financial situation and goals:

I. If You Want Stability: A fixed-rate mortgage is a good choice because your payments won't change.

II. If You Plan to Move Soon: An ARM might be better since the initial lower rate can save you money during the first few years.

III. If You Have Limited Savings: Look into FHA, VA, or USDA loans, which require smaller or no down payments.

IV. If You Want to Pay Less Interest: A shorter loan term, like 15 years, can save you money, but make sure you can handle the higher payments.

Shop Around and Compare Offers

Different lenders offer different rates and terms, so it's important to shop around. Get quotes from at least three lenders and compare them. Pay attention to:

- Interest rates and APR.
- Monthly payment amounts.
- Total costs, including fees and closing costs.

Ask questions if you're unsure about anything. A good lender will explain the details clearly so you can make the best choice.

Avoiding Predatory Lending Practices

When buying a home, it's important to be cautious about who you borrow money from. Some lenders use unfair practices, known as predatory lending, to take advantage of borrowers. These practices can leave you with loans that are too expensive, impossible to repay, or full of hidden fees. Knowing the warning signs and how to protect yourself can help you avoid these risks.

What Are Predatory Loans?

Predatory loans are designed to benefit the lender at your expense. They often come with very high-interest rates, hidden fees, or unfair terms that make it hard for you to pay back the money. These loans can cause serious financial trouble, including losing your home.

Warning Signs of Predatory Lending

Extremely High-Interest Rates

If a lender offers you an interest rate much higher than what other lenders are offering, it's a red flag. High-interest rates make your monthly payments more expensive and increase the total cost of the loan.

Hidden Fees

Predatory lenders may charge excessive fees that they don't explain upfront. Look out for fees labelled as "processing," "prepayment," or "document" fees. These can add thousands of dollars to your loan.

Pressure to Sign Quickly

If a lender rushes you to sign papers without giving you time to read or understand them, be careful. Honest lenders will let you take your time and ask questions.

Promises That Sound Too Good to Be True

A lender who says you're guaranteed to get a loan or promises approval without checking your credit score is likely untrustworthy. Legitimate lenders always review your finances before offering a loan.

Loan Terms That Keep Changing

If the loan terms, such as the interest rate or monthly payment amount, keep changing during the process, this could be a sign of a scam.

Balloon Payments

Some predatory loans have small monthly payments but include a large "balloon payment" at the end of the loan term. This can be impossible to pay and may lead to foreclosure.

Encouraging You to Borrow More Than You Can Afford

If a lender pushes you to take a bigger loan than you need or can afford, they may not have your best interests in mind.

How to Protect Yourself

Shop Around

Compare offers from multiple lenders. Look for clear terms and reasonable interest rates. Avoid working with lenders who pressure you into making a decision quickly. When shopping for a mortgage, it's important to understand the difference between banks and credit unions, as both offer loans but operate differently.

Banks

Banks are for-profit institutions that offer a variety of financial services, including mortgages. They are usually larger and have branches across the country, providing convenience and a wide range of loan options. However, because they are for-profit, their rates and fees might be slightly higher to maximize revenue for their shareholders. Banks often have more advanced online tools and services, making it easy to manage accounts digitally.

Credit Unions

Credit unions are not-for-profit organizations owned by their members. This means they often focus on providing better rates, lower fees, and personalized service to their members. Because they are member-focused, credit unions may offer mortgages with lower interest rates compared to banks. However, membership is usually required, and credit unions may have fewer branches and resources compared to large banks. They tend to have a more community-oriented approach and may prioritize customer relationships over profit.

Which Is Better?

The choice depends on your needs. If you value lower rates and personalized service, a credit union might be a better fit. If you want convenience, multiple branches, and a wide range of services, a bank could be the right choice. Comparing offers from both can help you find the best option for your situation.

Read Everything Carefully

Read all documents before signing. If you don't understand something, ask questions or have a trusted friend, family member, or lawyer review the papers with you.

Know Your Credit Score

Check your credit score before applying for a loan. This helps you understand what interest rate you qualify for, so you can spot offers that don't match your financial profile.

Use Reputable Lenders

Choose lenders with good reviews and a proven track record. Avoid companies that you've never heard of or that have complaints against them.

Look for Licensing

Make sure the lender is licensed to operate in your state. Most state licensing agencies have websites where you can verify this information.

Don't Borrow More Than You Need

Only take out a loan that fits your budget. Don't let a lender convince you to borrow more money or agree to monthly payments you can't handle.

4

Getting Pre-Approved for a Mortgage

Why Pre-Approval Matters

Getting pre-approved for a mortgage is one of the most important steps in buying a home. Pre-approval is when a lender reviews your finances and tells you how much they are willing to lend you. It shows that you're serious about buying a home and gives you an advantage over buyers who haven't been pre-approved. Let's break down why pre-approval matters and how it can help you.

What Is Pre-Approval?

When you apply for pre-approval, the lender checks your income, credit score, debt, and savings to determine how much money you can borrow. They give you a letter stating the loan amount you qualify for, the interest rate, and the loan terms. This letter is important because it tells sellers and real estate agents that you're financially ready to buy a home.

Pre-approval is different from pre-qualification. Pre-qualification is a quick estimate based on basic information, while pre-approval is a more detailed process that involves verifying your financial details. Pre-approval carries more weight because it's based on real numbers, not just guesses.

How Pre-Approval Strengthens Your Buying Power

Knowing Your Budget

Pre-approval helps you understand how much home you can afford. Instead of guessing, you'll have a clear idea of the price range you should look at. This saves time because you won't waste effort on homes that are too expensive.

For example, if you're pre-approved for a $250,000 loan, you can focus on homes within that range instead of looking at ones you can't afford.

Confidence in Making Offers

Sellers are more likely to take your offer seriously if you're pre-approved. It shows that you've already taken the first steps to secure financing and are ready to buy.

If you're competing with other buyers, being pre-approved gives you an edge. Sellers prefer buyers who are prepared and less likely to run into financing problems.

Faster Homebuying Process

When you're pre-approved, much of the loan process is already completed. This makes it faster to finalize the loan when you find a home you want to buy.

You'll also know the loan terms ahead of time, so there are fewer surprises during the closing process.

Stronger Negotiation Power

Pre-approval gives you more power during negotiations. Sellers are more likely to work with you if they know you've been pre-approved, which can lead to better deals or acceptance of your offer over others.

The Emotional Benefits of Pre-Approval

Buying a home can feel overwhelming, especially if you're not sure what to expect. Pre-approval reduces stress by giving you clarity and confidence. Knowing how much you can borrow and having a plan in place makes the entire process feel more manageable.

What You Need for Pre-Approval

To get pre-approved, you'll need to provide documents that show your financial situation. These include:

1. Proof of Income

Pay stubs, tax returns, or bank statements that show how much money you make.

2. Credit History

Lenders will check your credit score and report to see how well you've managed debt in the past.

3. Debt Information

Details about any debts you owe, like credit cards, car loans, or student loans.

4. Savings and Assets

Proof of savings or other assets that show you can afford the down payment and closing costs.

5. Employment History

A record of steady employment helps lenders see that you have a reliable source of income.

How to Use Your Pre-Approval Letter

Once you're pre-approved, you'll receive a letter from your lender. This letter can be shown to sellers and real estate agents as proof of your buying power. Here's how to use it:

1. Share It with Your Agent

Your real estate agent will use the pre-approval letter to show sellers that you're a serious buyer.

2. Include It with Your Offer

When you make an offer on a home, include the pre-approval letter. It gives sellers confidence that you can afford the home and close the deal.

When Does Pre-Approval Expire?

Pre-approval letters usually last for 60 to 90 days. If you don't buy a home within that time, you may need to get re-approved. It's important to keep your finances stable during this period. Avoid making large purchases, opening new credit accounts, or doing anything that could lower your credit score.

Documents Needed for Pre-Approval

Getting pre-approved for a mortgage is a big step toward buying your dream home. To get pre-approved, lenders need to see certain documents to understand your financial situation. These documents help them decide how much money they can lend you and whether you qualify for a loan. Here's a list of the most important documents you'll need to gather, explained in simple terms.

Proof of Income

Lenders need to know how much money you earn. This helps them decide if you'll be able to make monthly mortgage payments. You'll need to provide:

Pay Stubs

If you have a regular job, your most recent pay stubs (usually from the last two months) will show your earnings. They also confirm that you have a steady income.

Tax Returns

Lenders may ask for your tax returns from the past two years. These documents give a detailed view of your income and show if your earnings are consistent over time. Self-employed individuals especially need to provide tax returns to prove their income.

W-2 Forms

If you work for an employer, your W-2 forms from the last two years show how much you earned each year. This helps confirm the income listed on your pay stubs and tax returns.

Additional Income Proof

If you have other sources of income, such as freelance work, rental properties, or investments, provide documents like contracts or statements to show this income.

Credit History

Your credit history tells lenders how well you've managed money in the past. It includes your credit score and a detailed report of your borrowing and repayment habits. Here's what you need:

Credit Report

Lenders will check your credit report to see if you've paid bills on time, how much debt you owe, and how often you've borrowed money. They usually pull this information themselves, but you can request a free copy of your credit report beforehand to make sure it's accurate.

Explanation of Credit Issues

If you have any past problems, like late payments or accounts in collections, be prepared to explain them. Lenders appreciate honesty and may still approve your loan if you show improvement.

Bank Statements

Lenders want to see how much money you have in the bank. This helps them know if you can afford the down payment, closing costs, and other homebuying expenses. Provide:

Recent Bank Statements

You'll need to share statements from the past two to three months for all your bank accounts. These show how much money you have and whether your funds are stable.

Proof of Savings

If you've been saving money for a down payment, your bank statements will confirm this. Lenders like to see that you've been building your savings over time rather than receiving a sudden lump sum.

Gift Letters (if applicable)

If a family member or friend is giving you money for the down payment, you'll need a gift letter. This letter confirms that the money is a gift and not a loan that you'll have to pay back.

Employment Verification

Lenders need to know that your job is stable and reliable. They may contact your employer to confirm your position and salary. Be prepared to provide:

Employer Contact Information

Share your employer's name, address, and phone number so the lender can verify your job.

Work Contracts

If you're self-employed or work on a contract basis, provide copies of your contracts to show proof of ongoing work.

Personal Identification

To confirm your identity, you'll need to provide:

Government-Issued ID

A driver's license, passport, or other official identification is required.

Social Security Number

This is used to check your credit and verify your identity.

Tips for Organizing Your Documents

1. Create a Folder

   Gather all your documents in one place, either in a physical folder or a digital file. This keeps everything organized and easy to access.

2. Make Copies
   Make copies of important documents before submitting them to the lender. Keep the originals for your records.
3. Check for Accuracy
   Review all your documents to make sure there are no errors or missing information.

Why These Documents Are Important

Lenders use these documents to evaluate your financial health. They want to make sure you can afford the loan and are a trustworthy borrower. Providing accurate and complete documents speeds up the pre-approval process and increases your chances of getting approved.

Choosing the Right Lender

When buying a home, choosing the right lender is a crucial step. The lender is the financial institution or company that provides you with a loan to buy your home. Picking a trustworthy lender who fits your needs can save you money and make the process easier. Let's discuss how to research, compare, and choose the best lender for you.

Why the Right Lender Matters?

The lender you choose affects not only how much you pay but also your overall experience. A good lender offers fair rates, clear terms, and helpful support throughout the loan process. A poor choice can lead to higher costs, hidden fees, or unnecessary stress.

Step 1: Research Lenders

Start by learning about the different types of lenders available. These include:

1. Banks: Traditional banks offer mortgages, and they may provide benefits if you're already a customer.
2. Credit Unions: Credit unions often offer lower rates and fees, but you usually need to be a member to apply.
3. Mortgage Companies: These companies specialize in home loans and may offer more flexible options.
4. Online Lenders: Online lenders often have quick application processes and competitive rates.

Look at customer reviews and ratings for each lender to see how they treat their borrowers. You can find reviews online or ask friends and family about their experiences.

Step 2: Compare Loan Offers

Once you have a list of potential lenders, compare their loan offers. Request a Loan Estimate from each lender. This document shows you the details of the loan, including:

1. Interest Rate: This is the percentage you'll pay on top of the loan amount. A lower rate means lower monthly payments and less money spent over time.
2. Fees: Check for fees like application fees, origination fees, and closing costs. Some lenders may offer lower rates but charge higher fees.
3. Loan Terms: Compare the length of the loans (e.g., 15 years or 30 years) and decide which works best for you.
4. Monthly Payments: Make sure the payments fit your budget. Use the estimates to compare how much you'll pay each month.

Step 3: Check for Trustworthiness

A trustworthy lender should communicate clearly and be upfront about all costs. To ensure you're working with a reliable lender:

1. Verify Their Credentials: Check if the lender is licensed to operate in your state. You can usually find this information on your state's licensing website.
2. Ask Questions: A good lender will take the time to answer your questions. Ask about interest rates, fees, and any terms you don't understand.
3. Look for Transparency: Honest lenders will provide clear documents and avoid pressuring you to make decisions quickly.
4. Avoid Red Flags: Be cautious of lenders who promise approval without checking your finances or offer deals that seem too good to be true.

Step 4: Choose the Best Fit

After researching and comparing your options, choose the lender that offers the best combination of rates, terms, and service. Remember, the cheapest option isn't always the best. Consider the lender's reputation and how comfortable you feel working with them.

The Role of a Mortgage Broker

When buying a home, you might hear about mortgage brokers. A mortgage broker is a professional who helps you find a loan by connecting you with different lenders. They act as a middleman, working to match you with the best loan options based on your financial situation. While working with a broker can be helpful, it's important to understand both the benefits and the potential drawbacks.

What Does a Mortgage Broker Do?

A mortgage broker doesn't lend you money directly. Instead, they work with multiple lenders to find loans that meet your needs. They gather information about your finances, such as your income, credit score, and savings, and use this to find suitable loan options. Brokers can also help you compare different loans, explain complicated terms, and assist with paperwork.

Pros of Using a Mortgage Broker

Access to Multiple Lenders

One of the biggest advantages of using a broker is their wide network of lenders. Instead of applying to each lender yourself, the broker does the work of reaching out to different lenders and finding the best options for you.

Saving Time and Effort

Shopping for a mortgage on your own can be time-consuming. A broker simplifies the process by narrowing down the options and presenting the ones that fit your financial situation. This can save you a lot of time.

Expert Guidance

Brokers are experienced in the mortgage market and understand how different loans work. They can help explain the terms, interest rates, and fees, making it easier for you to understand your options.

Potentially Better Rates

Brokers often have access to special rates or deals from lenders that aren't available to the general public. This can help you secure a lower interest rate or better loan terms.

Help with Complicated Situations

If your financial situation is unusual, such as having a low credit score or irregular income, a broker can help find lenders who are willing to work with you. They know which lenders are more flexible and can match you with one that fits your needs.

Cons of Using a Mortgage Broker

Broker Fees

Brokers are paid either by you or the lender. If you're responsible for the fee, it can add to your upfront costs. Even if the lender pays the broker, the cost might be built into the loan, making it more expensive.

Potential for Bias

Some brokers may recommend lenders who pay them higher commissions, even if those loans aren't the best fit for you. It's important to ask your broker how they are paid and whether their recommendations are truly in your best interest.

Not All Lenders Work with Brokers

Some big banks and lenders don't work with brokers, so you might miss out on certain options. If you rely only on a broker, you could overlook a good deal from a lender they don't work with.

Less Control Over the Process

When working with a broker, you rely on them to handle the loan search and communication with lenders. This means you might feel less involved or informed about the process compared to handling it yourself.

Should You Work with a Mortgage Broker?

Deciding whether to use a broker depends on your situation. If you're new to home buying or have a complicated financial profile, a broker can make the process easier and help you find the right loan. On the other hand, if you prefer to research and compare lenders on your own, you might not need a broker.

5

Researching the Housing Market

Understanding Market Conditions

When buying a home, it's important to understand the housing market. The housing market changes based on factors like how many homes are for sale, how many buyers are looking, and the economy. Knowing these conditions can help you make smarter decisions and understand what to expect during your home search. Let's talk about the three main types of markets: buyer's market, seller's market, and balanced market.

What Is a Buyer's Market?

A buyer's market happens when there are more homes for sale than there are people looking to buy them. This means sellers are competing to attract buyers, which can work in your favour as a buyer.

In a buyer's market, home prices tend to be lower, and sellers may be more willing to negotiate. For example, you might be able to ask the seller to lower the price, include repairs, or cover some of your closing costs. Since there are plenty of homes available, you'll also have more options to choose from and less pressure to make a quick decision.

If you're buying in a buyer's market, take your time to find a home that meets your needs. Don't be afraid to negotiate for the best deal because sellers are eager to make a sale.

What Is a Seller's Market?

A seller's market is the opposite of a buyer's market. It happens when there are more people looking to buy homes than there are homes available. This gives sellers an advantage because buyers have to compete for a limited number of homes.

In a seller's market, home prices are usually higher, and homes sell quickly. Sellers might not be as open to negotiating because they know there are plenty of other buyers willing to pay the asking price. In some cases, multiple buyers might make offers on the same home, leading to bidding wars. This can make it harder to find a home within your budget.

If you're buying in a seller's market, it's important to act fast when you find a home you like. Be prepared to make a strong offer and stay flexible. You may need to prioritize what's most important to you, like location or home features, and be willing to compromise on other details.

What Is a Balanced Market?

A balanced market happens when there are about the same number of buyers and sellers. In this type of market, neither side has a big advantage, and prices tend to stay steady. Homes usually take a moderate amount of time to sell, and there's less pressure to make quick decisions.

In a balanced market, negotiations are more even. Sellers are open to reasonable offers, and buyers have a fair chance to find a home without feeling rushed. This type of market is ideal for both buyers and sellers because it creates a more stable and predictable environment.

If you're buying in a balanced market, take the time to compare homes and make a thoughtful decision. You're less likely to face extreme competition, but it's still important to stay within your budget and avoid overpaying.

How Market Conditions Affect Your Purchase

Market conditions play a big role in the homebuying process. Here's how each market type might affect your experience:

Price Negotiations

In a buyer's market, you have more room to negotiate the price and ask for repairs or other concessions. In a seller's market, you may need to offer the asking price or even more to secure the home.

Speed of Decision-Making

In a seller's market, you'll need to act quickly to make an offer before someone else does. In a buyer's market or balanced market, you'll have more time to think and compare options.

Inventory of Homes

A buyer's market offers plenty of choices, while a seller's market may leave you with fewer options. In a balanced market, you'll find a good variety without feeling overwhelmed.

Emotional Pressure

In a seller's market, the competition can feel stressful. Knowing the market conditions can help you stay realistic about what to expect and focus on finding the right home for your needs.

How to Research Market Conditions

To understand the housing market in your area, look at these key factors:

Home Prices

Check if prices are rising, falling, or staying steady. Rising prices often mean a seller's market, while falling prices suggest a buyer's market.

Days on Market (DOM)

This tells you how long homes are staying for sale. A short DOM usually indicates a seller's market, while a longer DOM suggests a buyer's market.

Inventory Levels

Look at how many homes are available for sale. A high number of listings means a buyer's market, while a low number of points to a seller's market.

Local Trends

Research the economy, job market, and population growth in the area. These factors can affect housing demand and market conditions.

Choosing a Location

Choosing the right location for your home is just as important as choosing the house itself. Where you live affects your daily life, from how long it takes to get to work to the kind of community you'll be part of. To make the best choice, think about these key factors: distance from work, local schools, safety, and community resources.

Proximity to Work

One of the first things to consider is how close your home will be to your workplace. A shorter commute can save you time, money, and stress. If you spend less time traveling to and from work, you'll have more time for family, relaxation, and hobbies.

Think about the type of transportation you'll use. Is the home close to public transportation, like buses or trains, if you need them? Or is it within a reasonable driving distance? Check the traffic patterns in the area to make sure your commute will be manageable, especially during rush hours.

Quality of Local Schools

If you have children or plan to in the future, the quality of nearby schools is an important factor. Even if you don't have kids, homes in areas with good schools often hold their value better and attract more buyers if you decide to sell later.

Research the schools in the area by checking their ratings, reviews, and performance reports. Visit the schools if possible, to get a sense of their environment. Also, consider how far the schools are from the home. A short and safe trip to school is always a plus.

Safety

Feeling safe in your new home is essential. Look into the crime rates in the neighbourhood to understand how safe it is. You can find this information online or ask local police departments for details.

Take a walk or drive through the neighbourhood during different times of the day to see how it feels. Are the streets well-lit at night? Do the homes and yards look cared for? These signs can give you a sense of the community's safety and upkeep.

Community Resources

Think about the things you'll need and use regularly, like grocery stores, hospitals, parks, and places of worship. Having these resources nearby makes life more convenient and enjoyable. For example, a local park can be a great place for children to play or for you to relax.

Consider the social aspects of the community, too. Are there community events, sports programs, or clubs that you might want to join? A neighbourhood with active community programs can help you feel connected and welcome.

Real Estate Trends and Timing Your Purchase

When you're buying a home, understanding real estate trends is important. These trends can affect how much you'll pay for a home, what your loan will cost, and how many houses are available for you to choose from. Learning about these patterns can help you decide when it's the best time to buy.

How Market Trends Affect Home Prices

Home prices go up or down based on the demand for homes and how many are available. If many people want to buy homes but there aren't enough houses for sale, prices will go up. This is called a seller's market because sellers have the upper hand—they can ask for higher prices, and buyers may have to pay more to compete.

On the other hand, if there are lots of homes for sale but not many buyers, prices usually go down. This is called a buyer's market because buyers have more options and can negotiate for better deals.

Pay attention to home price trends in the area where you want to buy. If prices have been rising quickly, it might be worth waiting until they level off. If prices are falling, it could be a good time to start looking for a home because you might find a better deal.

How Interest Rates Impact Your Purchase

Interest rates are another big factor in real estate trends. The interest rate is the percentage you pay to borrow money for your home loan. When interest rates are low, your monthly mortgage payments will also be lower, making it cheaper to buy a home.

For example, if you borrow $200,000 at a low interest rate, you'll pay less each month than if you borrow the same amount at a high rate. This means you can afford a more expensive home when rates are low. Many buyers rush to buy homes when interest rates drop because it makes owning a home more affordable.

When interest rates rise, fewer people can afford to buy homes, which can slow down the market. If rates are high, think carefully about whether you can afford the monthly payments or if it's better to wait for rates to come down.

How Inventory Affects Your Choices

Inventory refers to the number of homes available for sale. When inventory is low, there are fewer options for buyers. This often happens in a seller's market, where demand is high but supply is limited. In this situation, you may have to compete with other buyers for the same house, and sellers may not be willing to negotiate on price.

When inventory is high, there are more homes to choose from. This is common in a buyer's market, where sellers are eager to attract buyers. You'll have more options, and you may be able to negotiate a better price or ask for additional perks, like repairs or closing cost assistance.

Check how many homes are available in the area where you're looking. A local real estate agent can help you understand whether inventory is high, low, or average.

Timing Your Purchase

Timing your purchase means choosing the right moment based on real estate trends. Here are a few tips to help you decide:

Seasonal Trends

The housing market changes throughout the year. Spring and summer are usually busy because families like to move when kids are out of school. During this time, there are more homes for sale, but there's also more competition. Fall and winter are slower, so you might find better deals, but there may be fewer homes available.

Local Market Trends

Pay attention to what's happening in your area. Are home prices rising or falling? Are more homes coming on the market? Local trends can be different from national ones, so focus on the area where you want to buy.

Economic Conditions

Things like job growth, wages, and interest rates affect the real estate market. When the economy is strong, more people buy homes, which can drive up prices. When the economy slows down, prices may drop, making it a good time to buy.

Your Personal Situation

While market trends are important, the best time to buy is when you're financially ready. Make sure you have enough savings for a down payment, closing costs, and emergency funds. Don't rush into buying just because the market looks good—buy when you're fully prepared.

The Importance of Networking and Referrals

When you're looking to buy a home, having the right information can make the process easier. Networking and referrals are two of the best ways to learn about the local housing market and connect with trustworthy professionals. By building relationships and asking for recommendations, you can find valuable advice and avoid mistakes. Let's explore how networking and referrals can help and some tips to get started.

Why Networking Is Important

Networking is about connecting with people who can share helpful information or advice. When it comes to buying a home, these connections can include real estate agents, homeowners, friends, or family members. They can give you tips about neighbourhoods, recommend good professionals, and even let you know about homes that haven't been widely advertised yet.

For example, a homeowner in the area you like might tell you about a nearby property going on sale soon. A friend might recommend a reliable real estate agent who has helped others buy homes. These connections can save you time and help you make better choices.

Why Referrals Are Valuable

Referrals are recommendations from people you trust. When someone refers you to a professional, like a real estate agent or lender, it usually means they've had a good experience with that person. This helps you avoid working with someone who might not be reliable or knowledgeable.

Referrals also give you a starting point when you don't know where to begin. Instead of searching for professionals online and feeling overwhelmed by too many options, you can focus on the ones recommended by people you trust.

Tips for Networking

1. Talk to Family and Friends

   Start by asking family members, friends, or coworkers if they know any real estate agents or professionals they trust. They might also know someone who recently bought a home and can share their experiences.
2. Join Local Community Groups

   Look for online groups or forums related to the area where you want to buy a home. These groups often include homeowners and real estate professionals who can share local insights.
3. Attend Open Houses

   Open houses are a great way to meet real estate agents and other potential contacts. Even if you're not ready to buy, you can introduce yourself and ask questions about the area or the market.
4. Talk to Homeowners

   If you know people who already live in the area you're interested in, ask them about their experiences. They can tell you about the neighbourhood, local schools, and other important details.
5. Use Social Media

   Platforms like Facebook, Instagram, or LinkedIn can help you connect with local professionals and community groups. Many real estate agents share listings and market updates on these platforms, giving you a chance to learn more about them before reaching out.

Tips for Getting Referrals

1. Be Specific About What You Need

   When asking for referrals, be clear about what you're looking for. For example, if you need a real estate agent who specializes in first-time buyers, mention that. This helps the person giving the referral recommend the best fit for your needs.

2. Ask Multiple People
   Don't rely on just one referral. Ask several people for recommendations so you can compare options and choose the one that feels right for you.
3. Check Reviews and Credentials
   Even if someone refers you to a professional, take the time to check their reviews and credentials. Make sure they're licensed and have good feedback from past clients.
4. Follow Up
   When you get a referral, contact the professional and let them know who referred you. This helps build trust and makes the conversation more personal.

How Networking and Referrals Help with Local Insights

Local real estate professionals and homeowners have firsthand knowledge of the area. They can provide valuable insights, such as:

- Which neighbourhoods are family-friendly or close to work?
- Schools with good reputations.
- Upcoming developments that might affect home values.
- Market trends, like whether it's a buyer's or seller's market.

These insights are often more detailed and accurate than what you can find online, making them an important part of your decision-making process.

Building Long-Term Relationships

The people you connect with during your homebuying process can also help you in the future. For example, a good real estate agent can assist with selling your home later or finding a new one.

A homeowner you befriended might share tips about home maintenance or invite you to community events.

6

Working with Real Estate Professionals

Choosing the Right Real Estate Agent

When buying a home, especially for the first time, having the right real estate agent by your side can make a big difference. A real estate agent is a professional who helps you find homes, makes offers, and handles the paperwork involved in buying a house. As a first-time Black woman buyer, it's important to choose someone who understands your unique needs and supports you throughout the process. Here's how to find the right agent and what qualities to look for.

Why Choosing the Right Agent Matters?

Buying a home can feel overwhelming, especially when it's your first time. A good agent makes the process easier by guiding you, answering your questions, and helping you avoid mistakes. They understand the housing market, know how to negotiate, and can connect you with reliable lenders, inspectors, and other professionals. The right agent will be your partner, helping you make informed decisions.

Qualities to Look for in a Real Estate Agent

Experience and Knowledge

Look for an agent who knows the local housing market well. They should understand the area's home prices, neighbourhoods, and market trends. An experienced agent can help you find the best options within your budget and guide you through the buying process with confidence.

For example, if you're looking for a home in a specific neighbourhood, the agent should know about schools, safety, and nearby amenities. Their knowledge will help you make the best choice for your needs.

Good Communication Skills

Your agent should be a great communicator. They should listen to your needs, answer your questions clearly, and keep you updated every step of the way. A good agent explains complex terms in simple language and makes sure you understand what's happening.

If an agent is hard to reach or doesn't respond to your calls or emails, it may be a sign they're not the right fit.

Understanding of Your Unique Needs

As a first-time Black woman buyer, you may face unique challenges, like finding agents who respect your concerns or understanding programs that help minority buyers. Look for someone who values your perspective and takes the time to understand your goals.

A supportive agent will also be familiar with first-time buyer programs, grants, and loans designed to make homeownership more accessible.

Patience

First-time buyers often have many questions, and that's okay. A patient agent won't rush you into making decisions. Instead, they'll take the time to explain things and make sure you feel comfortable.

If you're unsure about a home or need more time to think, a patient agent will respect that and work at your pace.

Strong Negotiation Skills

Buying a home involves negotiation, whether it's about the price, repairs, or closing costs. A skilled agent knows how to negotiate on your behalf to get you the best deal possible. They should also know when to walk away from a deal if it's not in your best interest.

Trustworthiness

Your agent should be honest and transparent. They should explain all the costs involved in buying a home and make sure you're not caught off guard by hidden fees. A trustworthy agent will always prioritize your needs over their commission.

Where to Find a Real Estate Agent

1. Referrals
   Ask family, friends, or coworkers if they know any good agents. Personal recommendations are often the best way to find someone reliable and experienced.
2. Online Reviews
   Check online reviews and ratings for agents in your area. Look for feedback from other buyers, especially first-time buyers, to see if the agent is a good fit.
3. Local Real Estate Offices
   Visit local real estate offices and ask to meet agents. This gives you a chance to ask questions and see if their approach matches your needs.
4. Community Events
   Attend open houses or local events to meet agents in person. This can help you get a sense of their personality and professionalism.

Questions to Ask When Interviewing an Agent

Before choosing an agent, meet with a few and ask them questions to see if they're a good match. Here are some questions to consider:

1. How long have you been working as a real estate agent?
   Experience matters, especially in your local market.
2. Have you worked with first-time buyers before?
   An agent familiar with first-time buyers will understand the challenges you may face.

3. Do you have experience working with minority buyers or using first-time buyer programs?
   This ensures they can guide you toward resources and opportunities.
4. What's your approach to communication?
   Make sure they'll keep you informed and answer your questions promptly.
5. Can you provide references from past clients?
   Hearing from other buyers can give you confidence in their abilities.

How to Know You've Found the Right Agent

The right agent will make you feel comfortable, respected, and supported. They'll listen to your needs, work hard to find the best options, and keep your interests at heart. Trust your instincts—if something feels off or you don't feel fully supported, keep looking until you find the right fit.

Understanding the Agent's Role

A real estate agent plays an important role in helping you buy a home. They are there to guide you, answer your questions, and handle the complicated parts of the process. Whether it's finding the right house, negotiating the price, or completing paperwork, a good agent works to make the process smoother and less stressful for you. Let's take a closer look at what your agent should do for you.

Helping You Find the Right Home

One of the agent's main jobs is to help you find a home that meets your needs and fits your budget. They will ask you about your preferences, like the number of bedrooms, location, and any special features you want, such as a big backyard or a modern kitchen.

Using this information, your agent will search for homes that match your criteria. They will set up home tours so you can visit and see the houses in person. If you're not sure about a home, they can give advice and help you weigh the pros and cons.

Providing Market Knowledge

Your agent has knowledge about the local housing market. They can tell you whether a home is priced fairly and how it compares to similar homes in the area. They can also explain market trends, like whether home prices are rising or falling, and help you decide the best time to make an offer.

This information is especially useful for first-time buyers because it helps you avoid overpaying and understand what to expect.

Negotiating on Your Behalf

Once you find a home you like, your agent will help you make an offer. They will negotiate with the seller or their agent to get the best price and terms for you. If repairs are needed or if you want the seller to cover some of the closing costs, your agent will include these requests in the negotiations.

A skilled agent knows how to handle tough situations and can protect your interests throughout the negotiation process.

Handling the Paperwork

Buying a home involves a lot of paperwork, from contracts to legal forms. Your agent will handle this paperwork for you, ensuring that everything is completed correctly and on time. They will explain the documents so you understand what you're signing.

This includes the purchase agreement, inspection reports, loan documents, and closing forms. By taking care of the details, your agent helps you avoid mistakes that could cause delays or problems later.

Coordinating Inspections and Appraisals

Your agent will help schedule important steps like home inspections and appraisals. A home inspection checks for any problems with the house, like plumbing issues or roof damage. The appraisal determines the home's value, which is important for your lender to approve the loan.

If any issues come up during the inspection, your agent will help you decide how to proceed, such as asking the seller to make repairs or adjust the price.

Guiding You Through Closing

The closing is the final step in buying a home. Your agent will help you prepare for this step by reviewing the closing documents, ensuring all conditions of the sale are met, and answering any last-minute questions. They will also make sure you know what to expect on closing day, such as when and where to sign the final paperwork.

Providing Support and Advice

Throughout the process, your agent will be there to answer your questions and offer guidance. If you feel overwhelmed or unsure about something, they can provide reassurance and help you make confident decisions.

Negotiating Agent Fees and Contracts

When you hire a real estate agent to help you buy a home, they earn a fee for their services. This fee is usually a percentage of the home's price and is called a commission. While these fees are standard in the real estate market, it's important to understand them and know how to manage the costs. Here are some tips to help you negotiate agent fees and handle contracts wisely.

Understand How Agent Fees Work

Real estate agents are typically paid through a commission based on the final sale price of the home. For example, if the commission is 5% and the home costs $200,000, the total commission would be $10,000. This fee is usually split between the buyer's agent and the seller's agent.

In most cases, the seller pays the commission, which means the buyer doesn't pay the agent directly. However, it's still important to understand the fee structure since it affects the overall cost of the home.

Know What's Negotiable

Agent fees are not set in stone. While many agents have standard rates, these fees can sometimes be negotiated. For example:

Ask for a Lower Commission

If you're working with an agent who charges a higher commission, you can ask if they're willing to lower their fee.

Look for Discounts

Some agents offer discounts for first-time buyers, military families, or referrals from past clients. Ask if you qualify for any special rates.

Bundle Services

If your agent also helps with other tasks, like connecting you with a lender or handling extra paperwork, you might negotiate a package deal.

Not all agents will agree to lower their fees, but it's worth asking, especially if you're buying a higher-priced home.

Compare Multiple Agents

Before hiring an agent, meet with a few and ask about their fees and services. Some agents may charge lower fees while still offering excellent service. Comparing agents also helps you understand what's fair and reasonable in your area.

When comparing, don't focus only on the fees. Consider their experience, communication style, and knowledge of the market. A slightly higher fee might be worth it if the agent provides exceptional service.

Ask for a Clear Contract

Once you choose an agent, they will ask you to sign a contract that outlines their responsibilities and fees. This is called a buyer's representation agreement. Before signing, make sure the contract is clear and includes:

1. Commission Rate: The exact percentage or amount the agent will earn.
2. Duration of the Agreement: How long you'll work with the agent, typically 3 to 6 months.
3. Services Provided: Details about what the agent will do for you, like finding homes, negotiating, and handling paperwork.

If you see anything in the contract you don't understand, ask your agent to explain it. Don't be afraid to request changes if something doesn't seem right.

Avoid Hidden Fees

Some agents may include extra fees in the contract, like administrative fees or transaction fees. These are not standard and can often be negotiated or removed. Ask your agent upfront if there are any additional charges and get everything in writing.

Be Prepared to Walk Away

If an agent's fees seem too high or they're not willing to negotiate, don't be afraid to look elsewhere. There are many agents out there, and you have the right to work with someone who meets your needs and budget.

Value Good Service

While it's important to manage costs, remember that a good agent can save you money in other ways. They might negotiate a better price for your home or help you avoid costly mistakes. If an agent offers great service and support, their fee might be worth it in the long run.

Building Trust with Your Agent

When you're buying a home, your real estate agent is one of the most important people on your team. A strong and trusting relationship with your agent makes the process smoother, less stressful, and more enjoyable. Building trust with your agent isn't just about finding someone reliable—it's also about clear communication, mutual respect, and teamwork. Here's how to create a strong working relationship with your agent.

Be Honest About Your Needs

The first step in building trust with your agent is to be open and honest about what you're looking for in a home. Share your budget, your must-haves, and the things you can compromise on. If your agent has a clear understanding of your needs, they can focus on finding homes that match what you're looking for.

For example, if you want a home with three bedrooms, a backyard, and a short commute to work, let your agent know. If you have a strict budget, be upfront about it. Being honest from the start helps avoid misunderstandings later.

Communicate Clearly and Often

Good communication is key to a strong relationship. Make sure you're available to answer your agent's questions and respond to their messages. At the same time, don't be afraid to ask questions if you're unsure about something.

Let your agent know how you prefer to communicate, whether it's by phone, email, or text. Regular updates from both sides keep things moving smoothly and show that you're serious about buying a home.

Trust Their Expertise

Your agent is a professional with experience in the housing market. Trust their advice and guidance, especially when it comes to things like pricing, market conditions, and negotiations. They've likely helped many other buyers and know how to handle different situations.

For example, if your agent suggests making a strong offer on a home in a competitive market, listen to their reasoning. While you should always make decisions, you're comfortable with, trusting their expertise can help you avoid mistakes.

Respect Their Time

Real estate agents work hard to help their clients, often managing multiple buyers and sellers at once. Respect their time by being prepared for meetings, showing up on time, and letting them know if your plans change.

For instance, if you can't attend a scheduled home tour, inform your agent as soon as possible. Being respectful of their time shows that you value their efforts and helps build a positive relationship.

Be Patient and Flexible

Buying a home can take time, especially if the market is competitive or if you're looking for specific features. Be patient with your agent and understand that they're working hard to find the right home for you.

At the same time, stay flexible. If your agent suggests looking at homes outside your preferred area or slightly above your budget, consider their advice. Sometimes, being open to new ideas can lead to better options.

Address Concerns Early

If something isn't working in your relationship with your agent, speak up early. Whether it's a communication issue or a misunderstanding about your needs, addressing concerns right away helps avoid bigger problems later.

For example, if you feel your agent isn't showing you the type of homes you're interested in, explain what you're looking for in more detail. Most agents will appreciate your feedback and adjust their approach.

Show Appreciation

A little appreciation goes a long way in building trust. Thank your agent for their hard work and let them know you value their help. Whether it's finding the perfect home, negotiating a great deal, or answering all your questions, acknowledging their efforts helps create a positive working relationship.

Be a Team Player

Remember, buying a home is a team effort. Your agent is there to help you, but your involvement is just as important. Stay engaged in the process by reviewing listings, asking questions, and being proactive. When you work together as a team, the process becomes smoother and more enjoyable for both of you.

7

Exploring Your Housing Options

Types of Properties Available

When you're buying a home, there are different types of properties to choose from. Each type has its own pros and cons, so it's important to understand them before making a decision. The right choice depends on your lifestyle, budget, and long-term plans. Let's look at the most common types of properties: single-family homes, condos, townhouses, and multi-family units.

Single-Family Homes

A single-family home is a house built for one family. It sits on its own lot, meaning you won't share walls with neighbours. These homes often have a yard, garage, and more privacy compared to other property types.

Pros:

- Privacy: You have your own space without shared walls or common areas.
- Yard Space: Great for kids, pets, or gardening.
- Freedom: You can customize and renovate the home without needing approval from others.
- Resale Value: Single-family homes often hold their value well because they're in high demand.

Cons:

- Cost: They're usually more expensive to buy and maintain.
- Maintenance: You're responsible for all upkeep, like mowing the lawn, fixing the roof, and handling repairs.
- Space: While having a yard is great, it also means more work to keep it looking nice.

A single-family home is ideal if you want privacy and space for a family, but it requires more time and money for maintenance.

Condos

Condos, or condominiums, are individual units within a larger building or complex. You own your unit but share common areas like hallways, a pool, or a gym with other residents. Condos often have a homeowner's association (HOA) that manages maintenance and rules.

Pros:

- Lower Maintenance: The HOA takes care of exterior upkeep, like mowing the lawn or fixing the roof.
- Amenities: Many condos have shared facilities like pools, gyms, or clubhouses.
- Cost: Condos are often less expensive than single-family homes.

Cons:

- HOA Fees: You'll need to pay monthly fees to the HOA, which can add up.
- Rules and Restrictions: HOAs often have rules about things like pets, renovations, or parking.
- Less Privacy: Since you share walls and common spaces, it might feel less private.

Condos are a good choice for people who want less responsibility for maintenance and enjoy access to shared amenities. However, HOA fees and rules are something to keep in mind.

Townhouses

Townhouses are similar to single-family homes but are usually connected to other homes in a row. You own the interior, exterior, and sometimes a small yard, but you may also share walls with neighbours on one or both sides.

Pros:

- Affordability: Townhouses are often more affordable than single-family homes.
- Low Maintenance: Some townhouses have HOA services that handle exterior maintenance.
- Space: They usually have more space than condos, with multiple floors and sometimes a yard or garage.

Cons:

- Shared Walls: You might hear noise from neighbours, which reduces privacy.
- HOA Fees: If the townhouse is part of a HOA, you'll need to pay fees.
- Limited Customization: Like condos, there may be rules about what you can change on the exterior.

Townhouses are a middle-ground option, offering more space and privacy than condos but often at a lower cost than single-family homes.

Multi-Family Units

Multi-family units are buildings designed to house multiple families, such as duplexes, triplexes, or apartment buildings. You can live in one unit and rent out the others for extra income.

Pros:

- Income Opportunity: Renting out units can help you pay the mortgage or earn extra money.
- Shared Costs: If you own the whole property, you might split maintenance costs with tenants.
- Flexibility: You can live in one unit while having family members or tenants in the others.

Cons:

- Responsibility: You'll need to act as a landlord, which includes managing tenants and repairs.
- Shared Space: Even if you live on the property, you'll share common areas with others.
- Zoning Rules: Some areas have strict rules about multi-family properties, so you'll need to check local laws.

Multi-family units are a great option if you're interested in earning rental income, but they require more work and management.

Which Option Is Right for You?

Choosing the right property depends on your needs and priorities. Here are a few things to consider:

Budget:

Single-family homes and multi-family units are often more expensive upfront. Condos and townhouses may be more affordable, but HOA fees can add to your monthly costs.

Lifestyle:

If you value privacy and space, a single-family home might be the best fit. If you prefer less maintenance or want shared amenities, a condo or townhouse could be a better choice.

Future Plans:

If you're planning to grow your family, think about how much space you'll need. If you want extra income, a multi-family unit could be worth considering.

Location:

Some property types are more common in certain areas. For example, condos are often found in urban areas, while single-family homes are more common in suburbs.

New Construction vs. Existing Homes

When buying a home, one of the first decisions you'll need to make is whether to choose a newly built home or an existing one. Both options have their own benefits and challenges, and the right choice depends on your needs, budget, and timeline. Let's look at the key differences in cost, customization, and timelines to help you decide.

Cost Differences

One of the biggest factors to consider is cost. New construction and existing homes often differ in terms of price, but the true cost includes more than just the price tag.

New Construction Homes

Newly built homes are often more expensive than existing homes because they include modern features, energy-efficient materials, and the latest building technology. The base price of a new home might seem reasonable, but upgrades like flooring, countertops, and appliances can quickly add up.

However, new homes often have lower maintenance costs because everything is brand new. You're less likely to face major repairs, such as replacing a roof or fixing plumbing, for many years. Additionally, new homes may include warranties that cover certain repairs or issues for the first few years.

Existing Homes

Existing homes are usually less expensive upfront compared to new construction. However, they may require more maintenance or upgrades, such as replacing old appliances or repainting walls. Older homes may also have higher utility costs because they might not be as energy-efficient as newer ones.

On the other hand, existing homes often come with established landscaping, like mature trees and gardens, which can save you money compared to starting from scratch with a new build.

Customization Options

Another major difference is how much control you have over the design and layout of the home.

New Construction Homes

One of the biggest advantages of buying a new home is the ability to customize it. Many builders offer options for buyers to choose features like flooring, cabinets, countertops, and paint colours. You can often decide on the layout, number of bedrooms, or even add special features like a home office or a larger garage.

If you're building a home from the ground up, you can design it to perfectly fit your needs and preferences. However, these customizations can increase the overall cost, and some features might take longer to complete.

Existing Homes

When you buy an existing home, what you see is what you get. While you can remodel or make changes after purchasing, you won't have as much control upfront. For example, if you don't like the kitchen layout, you'll need to spend time and money to renovate it.

That said, existing homes often have unique features or charm that new homes might lack, such as original woodwork, unique architectural details, or a well-established style.

Timelines

The timeline for moving into your home is another important difference between new construction and existing homes.

New Construction Homes

Buying a newly built home often takes more time. If the home is already built but not yet sold, you might be able to move in quickly. However, if you're building a home from the ground up or making customizations, the process can take months or even a year. Delays can happen due to weather, supply chain issues, or changes in design.

If you're on a strict timeline or need to move quickly, a new construction home might not be the best option unless it's already completed.

Existing Homes

One of the biggest advantages of buying an existing home is that you can move in much faster. Once your offer is accepted and the paperwork is completed, you can usually move in within a few weeks to a couple of months. This makes existing homes a good option for people who need to relocate quickly or don't want to wait.

Energy Efficiency and Technology

New construction and existing homes also differ in terms of energy efficiency and modern technology.

New Construction Homes

New homes are built with the latest materials and technology, making them more energy-efficient. They often include features like better insulation, energy-efficient windows, and appliances designed to use less electricity or water. This can help lower your utility bills and make your home more comfortable.

Many new homes also include smart home technology, such as programmable thermostats, built-in security systems, or smart lighting.

Existing Homes

Older homes may not have the same level of energy efficiency or technology as new builds. You might need to spend money on upgrades, such as adding insulation, replacing windows, or installing energy-efficient appliances.

However, some existing homes may already have been updated by previous owners, so it's worth checking for features like solar panels or modern HVAC systems.

Location and Neighbourhood

The location of your home and the surrounding neighbourhood are important factors to think about.

New Construction Homes

New homes are often built in developing areas, which may not have the same amenities or infrastructure as older neighbourhoods. You might have to wait for schools, parks, or shopping centers to be built nearby. However, new developments often include modern designs, wider streets, and community amenities like pools or walking trails.

If you prefer a more suburban or rural setting, new construction might offer more options.

Existing Homes

Existing homes are usually in established neighbourhoods with mature landscaping, schools, and local amenities already in place. These neighbourhoods may have a sense of community and history that new developments lack.

If being close to schools, work, or public transportation is important, an existing home might be a better fit.

Resale Value

The resale value of your home is something to consider if you plan to sell it in the future.

New Construction Homes

New homes often have strong resale value because they include modern features and energy-efficient designs. However, if many new homes are built in the same area, it can create competition when you decide to sell.

Existing Homes

Older homes can hold their value well, especially if they're in a desirable neighbourhood or have unique features. Making updates or improvements can also increase the resale value.

Which One Is Right for You?

Choosing between a new construction home and an existing home depends on your priorities:

- If you want a home tailored to your tastes and don't mind waiting, a new construction home might be the best choice.
- If you need to move quickly or prefer an established neighbourhood, an existing home could be a better fit.
- Consider your budget, how much time you have, and whether you're willing to take on renovations or maintenance.

Evaluating Neighborhoods and Communities

Choosing the right neighbourhood is just as important as picking the right house. Where you live affects your daily life, your family's happiness, and your future goals. A good neighbourhood should match your lifestyle, support your plans, and provide a safe, comfortable environment for your family. To make the best choice, you'll need to research and evaluate different neighbourhoods carefully. Here's how to do it.

Think About Your Lifestyle

Start by considering what's most important to you and your family. Your neighbourhood should fit the way you live and the activities you enjoy. Ask yourself:

i. **Do You Need to Be Close to Work?**

A shorter commute can save you time and reduce stress. Check how far the neighbourhood is from your workplace and whether public transportation is available if you need it.

ii. **Do You Have Children or Plan to Have Them?**

If you have kids, look for neighbourhoods with good schools, parks, and activities for children. A family-friendly community can make life easier and more enjoyable for parents and kids.

iii. **Do You Prefer a Quiet or Busy Area?**

Some people like a peaceful neighbourhood with less traffic, while others enjoy the energy of a lively area with restaurants, shops, and entertainment nearby.

iv. **Do You Need Specific Amenities?**

Think about what's important to you, like grocery stores, gyms, libraries, or healthcare facilities. Having these nearby can make your daily life more convenient.

Research Local Schools

If you have children, the quality of schools in the neighbourhood should be a top priority. Even if you don't have kids, living near good schools can increase the value of your home over time. Here's what to look for:

- School Ratings and Reviews: Check online for ratings and reviews of schools in the area. A high rating often means the school provides good education and activities.

- Distance from the Home: Consider how far the school is from the neighbourhood. A shorter distance means an easier and safer commute for your kids.
- Extracurricular Activities: Look for schools that offer sports, arts, and other programs that match your child's interests.
- Community Feedback: Talk to parents in the neighbourhood to learn about their experiences with local schools.

Evaluate Safety

Safety is one of the most important factors when choosing a neighbourhood. You want to feel comfortable and secure in your new home. Here's how to assess safety:

- Check Crime Rates: Many websites provide crime statistics for neighbourhoods. Look for areas with low crime rates.
- Visit the Neighbourhood: Spend time walking or driving around the area at different times of the day. Pay attention to street lighting, cleanliness, and how well homes are maintained.
- Talk to Residents: Ask people who live in the neighbourhood about how safe they feel and whether they've experienced any issues.

Consider Future Growth

Think about how the neighbourhood might change in the future. An area that is growing or being developed can be a good investment, as property values may increase over time. Here's what to look for:

- New Construction: Are there new homes, schools, or businesses being built? This could indicate growth and potential for higher home values.
- Transportation Improvements: Plans for new roads or public transportation can make the area more accessible and desirable.

- Local Government Plans: Check if the local government has plans to improve parks, roads, or community facilities in the area.

Explore the Community Atmosphere

The overall vibe of the neighbourhood can make a big difference in your happiness. A strong sense of community can help you feel welcome and connected. Consider these factors:

i. **Are the Neighbours Friendly?**

   A welcoming community can make it easier to settle in. Look for neighbourhoods where people smile, greet each other, and seem engaged.

ii. **Are There Community Events?**

   Some neighbourhoods have block parties, farmers' markets, or other events that bring people together. This can be a great way to meet your neighbours and feel part of the community.

iii. **Are There Activities for All Ages?**

   A good neighbourhood should offer something for everyone, whether it's playgrounds for kids, walking trails for adults, or senior centres for older residents.

Check Property Values

The value of homes in the neighbourhood can tell you a lot about the area. Look for neighbourhoods where property values are stable or increasing. This shows that people want to live there, and it could mean a good return on your investment if you decide to sell later.

Look at Transportation and Accessibility

Good transportation options can make a neighbourhood more convenient. Check for:

- Public Transportation: If you don't drive, make sure the neighbourhood has buses, trains, or other options to get around.

- Road Conditions: Look at the roads and traffic patterns. Are they well-maintained? Is there heavy traffic during rush hours?
- Proximity to Major Roads: Being close to highways or main roads can make commuting easier, but too much traffic noise might be a downside.

Visit the Neighbourhood at Different Times

It's important to visit the neighbourhood during the day and at night. A neighbourhood that feels peaceful in the morning might feel different in the evening. Pay attention to:

- Noise Levels: Are there loud noises from traffic, trains, or neighbours?
- Activity: Are people outside walking, playing, or enjoying the area?
- Lighting: Is the neighbourhood well-lit at night? This can improve safety and comfort.

Talk to Local Residents

The people who already live in the neighbourhood can provide valuable insights. Ask them:

i. **What Do You Like About Living Here?**
   This can give you an idea of the area's strengths.
ii. **What Are the Downsides?**
   Honest feedback can help you avoid surprises.
iii. **Are There Any Community Rules or Associations?**
   Some neighbourhoods have homeowner's associations (HOAs) with rules about property maintenance or other issues.

Consider Your Long-Term Goals

Finally, think about how the neighbourhood fits into your future plans. If you're planning to grow your family, will the area still meet your needs in a few years? If you want to sell the home later, will the neighbourhood still be desirable?

First-Time Buyer Assistance Programs

Buying a home for the first time can feel overwhelming, especially when it comes to managing costs like the down payment and closing fees. Thankfully, there are programs designed to help first-time buyers, especially Black women and minority homebuyers, achieve their dream of homeownership. These programs offer grants, loans, and subsidies that make it easier to afford a home. Here's how you can find and apply for these resources.

What Are First-Time Buyer Assistance Programs?

First-time buyer assistance programs are created to help people buy their first home. They can provide financial help in different ways, such as:

i. Grants: Money given to you that you don't have to pay back.
ii. Loans with Low or No Interest: Special loans that make borrowing money cheaper.
iii. Subsidies: Financial aid to lower the cost of your home or mortgage payments.

These programs often focus on helping groups who face more challenges in buying a home, such as minorities, women, and low-income families.

How to Find Assistance Programs

Finding the right program can take a little research, but there are many resources available to help.

Start with Government Programs

- The federal government has programs to support first-time buyers, like the Federal Housing Administration

(FHA) loans and USDA loans. These are not granting but offer low down payments and easier credit requirements.

- Look into state and local government programs. Many states offer grants or low-interest loans specifically for first-time buyers.

Search for Non-profit Organizations

- Non-profit groups often run programs to help minority homebuyers. For example, the National Association of Real Estate Brokers (NAREB) focuses on increasing Black homeownership.
- Organizations like Habitat for Humanity or NeighborWorks America also provide affordable housing options and educational support.

Contact Housing Counsellors

- HUD-approved housing counsellors can guide you through the process of finding programs in your area. They also provide advice on budgeting and credit improvement.
- You can find a local housing counsellor through the U.S. Department of Housing and Urban Development (HUD) website.

Ask Your Real Estate Agent or Lender

- Real estate agents and mortgage lenders often know about local programs. They can connect you with resources tailored to your needs.

Search Online

- Websites like Down Payment Resource or HomePath Ready Buyer Program help you search for grants and programs based on your location and circumstances.

Programs Designed for Black Women and Minorities

Some programs specifically aim to support Black women and minority buyers. Here are a few examples:

The NAREB Homeownership Initiative

- This program provides education and access to resources to help Black families achieve homeownership.

State-Specific Minority Programs

- Many states have initiatives aimed at helping minorities, such as the California Housing Finance Agency (CalHFA) or Texas State Affordable Housing Corporation (TSAHC).

Specialized Loan Programs

- Some lenders offer loans with flexible terms for minority buyers. For example, Fannie Mae's HomeReady Program helps buyers with low to moderate income.

How to Apply for Assistance

Once you've found programs that interest you, follow these steps to apply:

Understand the Requirements

- Each program has specific requirements, like income limits, credit scores, or being a first-time buyer. Make sure you meet these criteria before applying.
- Some programs may require you to attend a homebuyer education course.

Gather Your Documents

- Prepare important documents, such as proof of income, tax returns, bank statements, and your credit report.
- If you're applying for grants or subsidies, you may need to provide additional paperwork showing your financial need.

Complete the Application

- Fill out the application carefully. Double-check all information to make sure it's accurate.
- Some applications can be done online, while others may require a visit to a local office.

Follow Up

- After submitting your application, stay in touch with the program to check the status. Respond promptly if they ask for more information.

Work with Your Lender

- If the program offers down payment assistance or subsidies, let your lender know. They can help incorporate these benefits into your mortgage.

Tips for Success

i. Improve Your Credit Score: Many programs require a minimum credit score. Check your score before applying, and take steps to improve it if needed, such as paying off small debts or correcting errors on your credit report.

ii. Save for Other Costs: Even with assistance, you'll need money for things like closing costs, moving expenses, and possibly repairs. Start saving early to cover these extras.

iii. Ask Questions: If you're unsure about any part of the process, ask for help. Housing counsellors, real estate agents, and lenders are there to assist you.

iv. Be Patient: Applying for assistance can take time, so be prepared for delays. Stay organized and keep track of deadlines.

8

The Home Search Process

Setting Your Priorities

When searching for your dream home, it's easy to get overwhelmed by all the options. Every house has different features, and not all of them will be a perfect fit. That's why it's important to clearly understand what you need and want in a home before you start looking. By creating a list of must-haves, nice-to-haves, and deal-breakers, you can stay focused on finding a home that fits your needs and budget. Let's explore how to set your priorities for a smoother home search.

Why Prioritizing Is Important

Buying a home is a big decision, and no home is 100% perfect. Some houses will have everything you want but cost too much, while others may fit your budget but lack some features. Prioritizing helps you focus on what matters most, so you can make a confident decision. It also saves time by helping you eliminate homes that don't meet your basic requirements.

Step 1: Understand Your Needs

Start by thinking about what you absolutely need in a home. These are your must-haves—the features that are non-negotiable. Without these, the home won't work for you or your family.

Here are some examples of common must-haves:

- Number of Bedrooms: How many bedrooms do you need for your family or future plans?
- Bathrooms: Do you need two bathrooms, or is one enough?
- Location: Do you need to live close to work, school, or public transportation?

- Budget: The home must fit within your financial limits.
- Safety: The neighbourhood must feel safe and have low crime rates.

Ask yourself: "What features can I not live without?" Write these down first to create your must-haves list.

Step 2: Think About Your Wants

Next, consider the features that you'd like to have but could live without if necessary. These are your nice-to-haves. They're not essential, but they can make your life more comfortable or enjoyable.

Examples of nice-to-haves might include:

- Extra Space: A guest room or a home office.
- Modern Kitchen: Granite countertops or stainless-steel appliances.
- Yard Size: A big backyard for kids or pets.
- Garage: Parking space for your car or storage.
- Community Amenities: A pool, gym, or park nearby.

Think of nice-to-haves as the features that would make you excited about a home but aren't deal-breakers if they're missing.

Step 3: Identify Deal breaker

Deal-breakers are the things that would make you reject a home, no matter what other features it has. These can include factors like safety, location, or specific home conditions.

Examples of deal-breakers might include:

- High Crime Rates

A neighborhood that doesn't feel safe or has a high crime rate could be a deal-breaker. Feeling secure in your home and community is essential for peace of mind.

- Bad School Districts

If you have children or plan to, living in an area with poorly rated schools may not be acceptable.

- Too Much Work Needed

A home requiring extensive repairs or renovations that exceed your budget might not be worth the investment.

- Traffic Noise

Homes near highways, busy roads, or other noisy areas might disrupt your quality of life.

Additional Considerations for Women of Color

For women of color, there are other factors to think about when identifying deal-breakers:

Demographic Diversity

Living in a neighborhood where you're the only person of your race or ethnicity can sometimes feel isolating or uncomfortable, especially if there's a lack of cultural understanding or support. Researching community diversity and visiting the area at different times can help you gauge how welcoming it feels.

Local Bias or Discrimination

Some neighborhoods may have a history of racial bias or exclusion. Understanding the area's history and reputation can help you avoid potential discomfort or hostility.

Access to Cultural Resources

For some, being near cultural centers, places of worship, or businesses that reflect their background and heritage can be important for maintaining a sense of belonging.

Supportive Community

Look for neighborhoods with active social networks, community organizations, or events that promote inclusion and diversity.

Step 4: Involve Everyone in the Decision

If you're buying a home with a partner, family, or roommates, it's important to involve them in the priority-setting process. Everyone may have different needs and wants, so discuss them together to create a shared list.

For example:

- Your partner may prioritize a big kitchen for cooking, while you value a quiet office space for working from home.
- Kids might prefer a backyard to play in or proximity to a school.

By involving everyone, you can make sure the home meets the needs of everyone living there.

Step 5: Use a Checklist

Creating a checklist is a great way to organize your priorities. Divide the checklist into three sections: must-haves, nice-to-haves, and deal-breakers. Here's an example:

Must-Haves:

- 3 bedrooms
- 2 bathrooms
- Within 30 minutes of work
- Safe neighbourhood
- Under $250,000

Nice-to-Haves:

- Fenced backyard
- Updated appliances
- Walk-in closet
- Hardwood floors

Deal-Breakers:

- Over budget
- Unsafe area
- Major structural issues

Use this checklist when visiting homes to see how well each property matches your needs.

Step 6: Stay Flexible

While it's important to know your priorities, remember that buying a home often involves compromise. You may not find a home that has everything on your nice-to-have list, but if it meets all your must-haves and avoids deal-breakers, it could still be a great fit.

For example, if you find a home that fits your budget, has the right number of bedrooms, and is in a safe area but doesn't have updated appliances, it might still be worth considering. Focus on the features that matter most to your daily life.

Step 7: Consider the Future

When setting your priorities, think about your long-term goals. Will the home still meet your needs in 5 or 10 years? For example:

- If you plan to start a family, consider whether the home has enough space for kids.
- If you're nearing retirement, look for a home that's easy to maintain and accessible.

Thinking ahead can help you avoid the hassle of moving again too soon.

Step 8: Work with Your Real Estate Agent

Share your priorities with your real estate agent. A good agent will use your list to find homes that match your needs and budget. They can also help you decide what's realistic based on the housing market in your area.

For example, if your must-haves include a large backyard and your budget is tight, your agent might suggest looking in neighbourhoods where homes are more affordable.

Step 9: Revaluate as Needed

As you start visiting homes, you may find that some of your priorities change. For example, you might realize that an extra bedroom is more important than a modern kitchen. That's okay—update your list as you go to reflect what you've learned.

House Hunting Tips

House hunting can be exciting but also overwhelming. With so many homes to choose from, it's important to stay organized and focused. Scheduling tours, reviewing listings, and attending open houses are all part of the process. Here are practical tips to help make house hunting easier and more enjoyable.

1. Set a Clear Plan Before You Start

Before you begin looking at homes, take some time to figure out your priorities. Know your budget, the type of home you want, and the neighbourhoods you're interested in. Create a list of must-haves, nice-to-haves, and deal-breakers. This will help you focus on homes that truly fit your needs.

For example:

- Must-haves: 3 bedrooms, 2 bathrooms, within 30 minutes of work.
- Nice-to-haves: Fenced backyard, modern kitchen, hardwood floors.
- Deal-breakers: Over budget, high crime rate, major repairs needed.

Having this plan will save you time by helping you skip homes that don't meet your basic requirements.

2. Review Listings Carefully

Online listings are a great way to get a first look at homes. Websites like Zillow, Realtor.com, or local real estate platforms show photos, descriptions, and details about homes for sale. Pay attention to:

- Price: Make sure the home is within your budget. Don't waste time looking at homes you can't afford.
- Location: Check the map to see if the home is in a good area for work, school, or other activities.
- Photos: Look at the pictures to get a sense of the home's condition and layout.
- Details: Read the description carefully to learn about the size, features, and any recent updates.

If a listing doesn't have enough information or photos, ask your real estate agent to find out more before scheduling a tour.

3. Schedule Tours Wisely

When you find homes you like, schedule tours to see them in person. Here are some tips to make the most of your time:

- Plan Ahead: Try to schedule multiple tours on the same day if the homes are close to each other. This saves time and allows you to compare homes more easily.
- Be Flexible: Some homes may only be available for tours at specific times, so be ready to adjust your schedule.
- Allow Enough Time: Give yourself enough time to explore each home without feeling rushed. Plan for at least 30 minutes per home.

Your agent can help coordinate the tours and make sure you have access to the homes.

4. Take Notes During Tours

It's easy to forget details about a home after you've seen a few. Bring a notebook or use your phone to jot down notes during each tour. Write about what you liked, what you didn't, and any questions you have.

For example:

- What I Liked: Spacious kitchen, quiet neighborhood, large windows.
- What I Didn't Like: Small closets, outdated bathrooms.
- Questions: How old is the roof? Are appliances included?

Taking photos (if allowed) can also help you remember details later.

5. Don't Skip Open Houses

Open houses are a great way to see homes without scheduling a tour. They're usually held on weekends and allow potential buyers to explore the property freely. Here's how to make the most of an open house:

- Arrive Early: Arriving at the beginning gives you more time to look around before it gets crowded.
- Ask Questions: The agent hosting the open house can answer questions about the home, such as its history or the seller's timeline.
- Observe Other Buyers: Watching how others react to the home can give you an idea of its popularity and whether you might face competition.

Even if you're not sure about a home, attending an open house can help you get a better sense of what you're looking for.

6. Pay Attention to the Details

During tours and open houses, it's important to look beyond the surface. While the paint colours or furniture might catch your eye, focus on things that matter in the long term, such as:

- Condition of the Home: Look for signs of damage, like cracks in the walls, water stains, or uneven floors.

- Storage Space: Check closets, cabinets, and storage areas to see if they meet your needs.
- Layout: Think about whether the layout works for your lifestyle. For example, is the kitchen easy to access from the living room?
- Neighborhood Noise: Listen for traffic, barking dogs, or other noise that might affect your comfort.

7. Stay Realistic

It's easy to fall in love with a home that looks perfect, but be realistic about whether it truly fits your needs and budget. Don't stretch your finances just to get a home with extra features you don't really need.

For example, if a home has a beautiful pool but is far from work or over budget, it might not be the best choice. Focus on homes that meet your most important priorities.

8. Ask Your Agent for Advice

Your real estate agent is a valuable resource during house hunting. They know the market and can help you understand things like:

- Whether the home is priced fairly.
- What repairs or updates might be needed?
- How much competition there is from other buyers.

Don't hesitate to ask for their opinion or guidance if you're unsure about a home.

9. Take Your Time

While it's important to act quickly in a competitive market, don't rush into a decision. Buying a home is a big commitment, so make sure you're confident in your choice. If a home doesn't feel right, trust your instincts and keep looking.

10. Review Your Options

After visiting several homes, take some time to review your notes and compare them. Think about how each home matches your priorities and which one feels like the best fit. Discuss your options with your family or partner to make a decision together.

Virtual Tours and Digital Tools

Finding a home has become much easier thanks to online platforms, virtual tours, and mobile apps. These tools let you explore homes, learn about neighbourhoods, and compare properties from the comfort of your home. Whether you're a first-time buyer or someone looking for their next home, using these tools wisely can save you time and help you make better decisions. Let's look at how to make the most of them.

Understanding Online Home Search Platforms

Online home search platforms like Zillow, Realtor.com, and Redfin are great for browsing homes for sale. These websites give you access to pictures, descriptions, and details about each property. Here's how to use them effectively:

Use Filters

Most platforms let you filter your search. You can set preferences for price range, number of bedrooms, location, and more. This helps you focus only on homes that match your needs.

Check Photos

Look carefully at the photos provided. Pay attention to details like flooring, kitchen appliances, and overall condition. Sometimes, photos can make a space look better than it really is, so focus on practical aspects.

Read the Description

Descriptions often include details you can't see in photos, like the size of the yard, recent updates, or special features like a fireplace or walk-in closet.

Look at the Map

Many platforms include maps showing where the property is located. Use this to check if the home is near schools, stores, or public transportation.

Making the Most of Virtual Tours

Virtual tours are an exciting feature that lets you explore a home without physically visiting it. They give you a 360-degree view of each room, allowing you to imagine yourself in the space. Here's how to get the most out of virtual tours:

Explore Every Room

Don't just look at the main areas like the living room or kitchen. Check bedrooms, bathrooms, closets, and other spaces to get a complete picture.

Zoom in on Details

Virtual tours often let you zoom in. Use this to check the condition of walls, flooring, or fixtures like light switches and faucets.

Check the Layout

A virtual tour can help you understand how the rooms are connected. Is the kitchen close to the dining room? Are the bedrooms on the same floor? The layout should match your needs.

Take Notes

Jot down your thoughts about the home during the tour. For example, write what you like about the space and what concerns you might have, like small storage areas or old-looking appliances.

Using Mobile Apps for House Hunting

Mobile apps like Zillow, Trulia, and Redfin make house hunting even easier. You can use them on the go to browse listings, save your favourites, and get notifications about new homes. Here are some tips for using apps effectively:

Set Alerts

Apps let you create alerts for homes that match your criteria. This way, you'll get notified as soon as a new listing becomes available.

Save Listings

Save the homes you like so you can compare them later. Many apps let you create a list of favourites to keep everything organized.

Use the Map View

Most apps have a map view that shows where each home is located. You can see nearby schools, parks, or stores, which helps you learn more about the neighborhood.

Check Open Houses

Apps often include information about open houses. You can use this feature to plan visits if you want to see a home in person.

Comparing Homes Online

Once you've found a few homes you like, it's important to compare them to see which one fits your needs best. Here's how to do it:

Create a Spreadsheet

List each home's details, like price, size, number of bedrooms, and key features. Include a column for pros and cons to help you make a decision.

Use Side-by-Side Comparison Tools

Some platforms let you compare homes side by side. This can be helpful for seeing differences in price, condition, or features.

Rank Your Options

After reviewing all the details, rank the homes based on how well they meet your needs. This will make it easier to decide which ones to focus on.

Questions to Ask About Online Listings and Tours

While online tools are helpful, they can't tell you everything about a home. Be ready to ask questions about things that might not be clear from the listing or tour:

- Condition of the Home:
  Are there any issues with the plumbing, roof, or foundation?
- Neighborhood:
  Is the area safe? Are there any nearby parks or schools?
- Age of Appliances:
  How old are the appliances, and are they included in the sale?
- Extra Costs:
  Are there HOA fees or any other costs you should know about?

Your real estate agent can help answer these questions or get more information from the seller.

Pros and Cons of Virtual Tools

Like anything, virtual tools have their advantages and disadvantages.

Pros:

- Save time by narrowing down options without visiting every home.
- Explore homes in other cities or states if you're relocating.
- Get a good idea of the layout and space before scheduling a tour.

Cons:

- Photos and virtual tours might not show everything, like odors or noises.

- You can't experience the neighborhood atmosphere online.
- Some listings may not be up to date, leading to confusion.

Combine Virtual Tools with In-Person Visits

While online tools are great, they shouldn't replace in-person visits completely. After narrowing down your options, plan to visit your favorite homes to confirm they meet your expectations.

For example:

- If the virtual tour showed a spacious backyard, visit in person to see if it's really as big as it looks.
- If the listing says the home is in a quiet area, check the neighborhood at different times of the day to ensure it meets your preferences.

Stay Safe Online

When using online tools, make sure you're browsing reputable websites and apps. Be cautious about sharing personal information, like your credit score or financial details, until you're working with a verified agent or lender.

Evaluating a Home's Condition

When looking at a home, it's important to check its condition carefully. This helps you avoid surprises and costly repairs later. Even if a home looks beautiful on the surface, there could be hidden problems with the structure, plumbing, electrical systems, or other parts of the house. Here are key things to look for during a home viewing to make sure it's in good shape.

Check the Structure

The structure of a home is its foundation and frame. It keeps the house strong and stable, so any issues here can lead to big problems. Look for these signs when inspecting the structure:

- Cracks in Walls or Ceilings:
  Small cracks are common, but large or uneven cracks might mean foundation issues.
- Uneven Floors:
  If the floors slope or feel bouncy, it could be a sign of structural problems.
- Doors and Windows:
  Open and close all doors and windows. If they stick or don't fit properly, it might mean the foundation has shifted.
- Water Damage:
  Look for stains on walls, ceilings, or floors. This could mean there's a leak in the roof or foundation.

If you notice any of these issues, ask the seller or real estate agent for more information. A professional inspection can confirm whether the problems are serious.

Inspect the Roof

The roof protects the home from weather, so it's important to make sure it's in good condition. Here's what to check:

- Shingles:
  Look at the shingles from the ground. Are any missing, cracked, or curling?
- Age of the Roof:
  Ask how old the roof is. Most roofs last 20–30 years, depending on the material.
- Leaks:
  Look for signs of water damage inside the house, especially in the attic or near the ceilings. This could mean the roof is leaking.

A damaged roof can be expensive to replace, so it's important to know its condition before buying.

Test the Plumbing

Good plumbing is essential for a home to function properly. Here's what to check during a viewing:

- Water Pressure:

  Turn on faucets in the kitchen and bathrooms. Make sure the water flows steadily and doesn't sputter.
- Leaks:

  Look under sinks for puddles or drips. Also, check for water stains on walls or ceilings.
- Toilets:

  Flush the toilets to see if they work properly and refill quickly.
- Water Heater:

  Ask about the age of the water heater. Most last 8–12 years, so an older unit might need replacing soon.

Plumbing repairs can be costly, so it's a good idea to identify potential problems early.

Examine the Electrical Systems

Electrical systems power your home and keep it safe. Faulty wiring can be dangerous, so check for these signs:

- Outlets and Switches:

  Test outlets and light switches to make sure they work. Look for outlets with burn marks or loose covers, which could mean wiring problems.
- Circuit Breaker Panel:

  Open the breaker panel and check for labels. A well-labelled panel shows the system is organized. If it looks messy, it might need updating.
- Flickering Lights:

  Flickering or dimming lights can indicate electrical issues.

- GFCI Outlets:
  Bathrooms and kitchens should have GFCI (ground fault circuit interrupter) outlets for safety. These outlets have reset buttons and protect against electrical shocks.

If you have concerns about the electrical system, a licensed electrician can perform a detailed inspection.

Look for Signs of Pests

Pests like termites, ants, or rodents can cause serious damage to a home. During your viewing, check for these warning signs:

- Chewed Wires or Wood:
  Look at baseboards, window sills, and wooden beams for signs of chewing or holes.
- Droppings:
  Small droppings in corners or cabinets could mean rodents are present.
- Mud Tubes:
  Termites often build mud tubes along walls or foundations.
- Odd Smells:
  Unusual odors in the basement or attic might indicate pest problems.

If you spot signs of pests, consider having a pest inspection done before making an offer.

Inspect the HVAC System

The heating, ventilation, and air conditioning (HVAC) system is crucial for keeping your home comfortable. Here's what to check:

- Furnace and AC Unit:
  Ask about the age and maintenance history of the furnace and air conditioner. Most systems last 15–20 years.

- Air Vents:
  Make sure vents are clean and not blocked.
- Thermostat:
  Test the thermostat to ensure it works properly and controls the temperature.

Replacing an HVAC system can be expensive, so it's good to know if it's in good working order.

Examine Windows and Doors

Windows and doors affect the home's energy efficiency and security. Check these things:

- Drafts:
  Feel around windows and doors for cold air. Drafts can increase energy bills.
- Locks:
  Test locks on all windows and doors to ensure they're secure.
- Glass Condition:
  Look for cracks or fogging between double-pane windows. This could mean the seal is broken.

Look at the Basement and Attic

Basements and attics can reveal a lot about a home's condition. Here's what to look for:

- Basement:
  Check for moisture, musty smells, or water stains, which could mean the foundation leaks.
- Attic:
  Look for proper insulation and ventilation. Also, check for signs of pests or roof leaks.

Don't Ignore the Exterior

The outside of the home is just as important as the inside. Pay attention to:

- Siding or Paint:
  Look for peeling paint or damaged siding.
- Driveway and Walkways:
  Check for cracks or uneven surfaces.
- Gutters and Downspouts:
  Make sure gutters are clear and direct water away from the home.

Ask for a Professional Inspection

Even if everything looks good during your viewing, it's a smart idea to hire a professional inspector. They can check for hidden issues and give you a detailed report on the home's condition.

9

Making an Offer and Negotiating

Understanding the Offer Process

Making an offer on a home is an important step in becoming a homeowner. It shows the seller that you are serious about buying their property. However, the process involves more than just stating a price. You'll need to follow certain steps, consider counteroffers, and negotiate to get the best deal. Let's break down how to make an offer, handle counteroffers, and negotiate the price in simple terms.

Getting Ready to Make an Offer

Before making an offer, it's important to be prepared. This starts with knowing how much you can afford. Talk to your lender and get pre-approved for a mortgage. This means the lender has checked your financial information and agrees to lend you a certain amount. A pre-approval letter shows the seller that you're serious and ready to buy. Next, research the market. Look at homes in the area that are similar to the one you're interested in. These are called "comparable" or "comps." They help you understand if the home is priced fairly. Lastly, talk to your real estate agent about your offer. They will guide you on what price to start with and what terms to include.

What Your Offer Includes

Your offer is a formal document, often called a purchase agreement, that outlines the terms of the sale. It includes the price you're willing to pay, the closing date (when you want to complete the purchase), and any contingencies. Contingencies are conditions that must be met for the deal to go through. Common contingencies include a home inspection, the ability to secure financing, or the home appraising for the agreed-upon price. You'll also include earnest money in your offer. This is a small deposit that shows the seller you're serious. If the deal goes through, the earnest money will go toward your down payment. If not, you may get it back depending on the terms of your contract.

Submitting the Offer

Once your offer is ready, your real estate agent will present it to the seller's agent. The seller will then review it and decide how to respond. It's common to feel nervous during this waiting period, but remember that this is a normal part of the process. The seller has three options: they can accept your offer, reject it, or make a counteroffer.

When the Seller Accepts

If the seller accepts your offer, congratulations! This means they agree to all the terms, including the price and contingencies. Both parties will sign the purchase agreement, and the home will go under contract. At this point, you'll begin working on the next steps, such as scheduling a home inspection and finalizing your mortgage.

When the Seller Rejects

If the seller rejects your offer, don't be discouraged. Rejection doesn't always mean the seller isn't interested in selling to you. It could mean your offer was too low, or they have other offers to consider. Talk to your real estate agent about whether you should make a new offer with different terms or move on to another home.

Handling Counteroffers

If the seller makes a counteroffer, they are suggesting changes to your original offer. Common changes include increasing the price, changing the closing date, or removing contingencies. When you receive a counteroffer, you have three options: you can accept it, reject it, or make a counteroffer of your own. Counteroffers can go back and forth several times until both parties reach an agreement.

For example, let's say you offered $200,000, but the seller countered with $210,000. You could accept their price, offer $205,000 as a compromise, or stick with your original offer and see if they agree. This back-and-forth negotiation is normal and helps ensure that both you and the seller feel satisfied with the deal.

Negotiating the Price

Negotiating is a key part of the home-buying process. Your real estate agent will be your biggest ally during this step. They have experience in negotiating and can help you get the best deal. When negotiating, it's important to stay respectful and flexible. The seller wants to get a good price for their home, just as you want to get a fair deal.

If you're in a buyer's market, where there are more homes for sale than buyers, you may have more room to negotiate. In a seller's market, where homes sell quickly and there's a lot of competition, you may need to offer closer to the asking price or even above it. Be realistic about your budget and what the home is worth. Don't stretch your finances just to win the deal.

Contingencies and Their Role in Negotiation

Contingencies can also play a role in negotiations. For example, if you include a contingency for a home inspection, you can negotiate repairs or ask for a credit if the inspection reveals problems. Similarly, if the home appraisal comes back lower than the agreed price, you can negotiate to lower the price to match the appraisal.

Keep in mind that sellers prefer fewer contingencies because they make the sale process smoother. If you're confident about the home's condition or your financing, you might consider waiving some contingencies to make your offer more attractive. However, always discuss this with your real estate agent to ensure it's a safe choice.

Staying Calm and Patient

Negotiations can take time, especially if there are counteroffers involved. It's important to stay calm and patient during this process. Remember, you don't have to agree to terms that make you uncomfortable. If the seller isn't willing to meet your needs, it's okay to walk away and look for another home.

Finalizing the Agreement

Once both you and the seller agree on the terms, you'll finalize the purchase agreement. This document becomes a binding contract, and you'll move on to the next steps in the home-buying process. These steps include completing the home inspection, securing your mortgage, and preparing for closing.

Competing in a Seller's Market

In a seller's market, there are more buyers than homes available. This creates a lot of competition, and sellers often receive multiple offers on their property. If you're buying a home in this type of market, it's important to make your offer stand out. While it might feel challenging, there are ways to improve your chances of winning the home you want. Here are tips to help you make a strong offer when competition is high.

1. Get Pre-Approved for a Mortgage

Before you start making offers, get pre-approved for a mortgage. A pre-approval letter shows sellers that you're a serious buyer who can afford the home. It also gives you an advantage over buyers who are only pre-qualified or haven't talked to a lender yet. Pre-approval tells the seller that financing won't delay the process, which makes your offer more attractive.

2. Offer a Competitive Price

In a seller's market, you might not have the option to negotiate a lower price. Homes often sell at or above the asking price because of high demand. Look at similar homes in the area to understand what they're selling for and offer a fair, competitive price. If the house is priced right, offering too little could make your offer less appealing and result in the seller choosing someone else.

3. Increase Your Earnest Money Deposit

Earnest money is the deposit you include with your offer to show you're serious about buying the home. In a competitive market, offering a larger deposit can make your offer more attractive. This shows the seller that you're committed and willing to put more money on the line. If the deal goes through, the earnest money will go toward your down payment, so it's not extra money you'll lose.

4. Keep Contingencies Minimal

Contingencies are conditions that must be met for the sale to happen. Common contingencies include home inspections, appraisals, or the ability to secure financing. While these are important protections for buyers, too many contingencies can make your offer less appealing in a seller's market. Sellers want a smooth and quick sale, so they may choose offers with fewer conditions.

If you're confident about the home and your financial situation, consider waiving some contingencies to strengthen your offer. For example, you might waive the inspection contingency if you've had a chance to review the property thoroughly. However, always discuss this with your real estate agent to ensure it's a safe choice.

5. Be Flexible with the Closing Date

Sometimes, flexibility can make your offer stand out. Ask your real estate agent about the seller's needs. If they're in a hurry to sell, offering a quick closing might work in your favour. On the other hand, if they need more time to move out, offering to delay the closing could make your offer more attractive. Being flexible shows the seller that you're willing to accommodate their situation.

6. Include a Personal Touch

Adding a personal letter with your offer can make a big difference. Write a short, heartfelt note to the seller explaining why you love the home and how you see yourself living there. Sellers are often emotionally attached to their homes, and knowing their property will go to someone who will care for it can sway their decision. Be genuine and sincere in your letter, but avoid making promises you can't keep.

7. Escalation Clause

In a competitive market, an escalation clause can help your offer stand out without overpaying from the start. This clause states that you're willing to increase your offer by a specific amount if someone else offers more, up to a maximum price. For example, if the asking price is $300,000 and another buyer offers $310,000, your escalation clause could automatically increase your offer to $315,000. This shows the seller you're serious without committing to an unnecessarily high price.

8. Work with an Experienced Agent

Having a knowledgeable real estate agent is crucial in a seller's market. They understand how to craft strong offers and can guide you through the process. An experienced agent knows the local market, has connections with other agents, and can help you move quickly when opportunities arise. They'll also help you decide what terms and strategies will make your offer more competitive.

9. Avoid Asking for Extras

In a seller's market, avoid asking for extras that might make your offer less appealing. For example, don't request that the seller cover closing costs or leave behind furniture unless absolutely necessary. Keeping your offer simple shows the seller that you're easy to work with and focused on the purchase itself.

10. Be Prepared to Move Quickly

Homes sell fast in a seller's market, so you need to act quickly. If you find a home you like, don't wait too long to make an offer. Have your paperwork ready and stay in close contact with your real estate agent. Being prepared to move quickly can give you an edge over buyers who hesitate.

11. Consider Paying in Cash (If Possible)

If you have the ability to pay in cash, this can make your offer much more attractive. Cash offers eliminate the need for financing, which reduces the chances of delays or complications. Even if you can't pay the full amount in cash, offering a larger down payment can still show the seller that you're financially secure.

12. Stay Positive and Persistent

In a seller's market, it's common to face rejection or lose out to other buyers. Don't get discouraged. Stay focused on your goals and keep looking for homes that fit your needs. With patience and persistence, the right home will come along, and you'll be ready to make a strong offer.

Contingencies and Conditions

When buying a home, including contingencies in your offer is an important step. Contingencies are conditions that must be met for the sale to go through. They protect you as the buyer, ensuring you can back out of the deal if something unexpected happens, without losing your earnest money. Some of the most common contingencies are inspection, financing, and appraisal contingencies. Each one plays a vital role in making sure your home purchase is safe and smart. Let's explore why they matter and how they work.

What Are Contingencies?

A contingency is like a safety net in your offer. It means the sale of the home depends on specific conditions being met. If these conditions aren't met, you have the right to cancel the purchase without losing the earnest money you've put down. Think of contingencies as a way to protect your investment and avoid surprises.

Inspection Contingency

The inspection contingency allows you to have the home inspected by a professional before finalizing the deal. This is one of the most important contingencies because it helps you uncover any hidden problems with the house.

When you include an inspection contingency, you're essentially saying, "I want to buy this home, but only if it passes a professional inspection." If the inspector finds major issues, such as a leaky roof, plumbing problems, or electrical issues, you can ask the seller to fix them, lower the price, or even cancel the deal.

Here's why the inspection contingency is crucial:

- Avoid Costly Repairs: Inspections help you spot problems early. Fixing things like a damaged foundation or faulty wiring can be very expensive.
- Negotiation Power: If the inspection reveals problems, you can negotiate with the seller to address them. For example, the seller

might agree to repair the issue or lower the price to cover the cost of fixing it yourself.

- Peace of Mind: Knowing the home is in good condition allows you to move forward confidently.

Skipping the inspection contingency can be risky, as you might end up buying a home with costly repairs that you didn't plan for.

Financing Contingency

The financing contingency protects you in case your mortgage loan isn't approved. Even if you're pre-approved for a loan, there's still a chance something could go wrong during the final approval process. For example, the lender might discover a credit issue or decide the home's value doesn't match the loan amount.

When you include a financing contingency, you're saying, "I want to buy this home, but only if I can secure a loan." If your loan is denied, the contingency allows you to cancel the purchase and get your earnest money back.

Here's why the financing contingency is important:

- No Financial Risk: Without this contingency, you could lose your earnest money if your loan doesn't get approved.
- Protects Your Budget: If the loan terms change (e.g., higher interest rates), you can back out if the new terms are no longer affordable.
- Gives You Time: This contingency gives you a specific amount of time to secure financing, ensuring you don't feel rushed.

While sellers prefer offers without financing contingencies, it's a vital safeguard for most buyers unless you're paying in cash.

Appraisal Contingency

The appraisal contingency ensures the home's value matches the agreed price. Before a lender approves your mortgage, they will order an appraisal to determine the home's fair market value. If the appraisal comes in lower than the price you agreed to pay, the lender might not approve the full loan amount.

For example, if you agree to buy a home for $300,000 but the appraisal says it's only worth $280,000, your lender will likely offer a loan based on the $280,000 value. Without an appraisal contingency, you'd have to cover the $20,000 difference out of your pocket—or risk losing your earnest money if you back out of the deal.

Here's why the appraisal contingency matters:

- Fair Value: It ensures you're not overpaying for the home.
- Financial Protection: If the appraisal is lower than the purchase price, you can negotiate with the seller to lower the price or cancel the deal.
- Helps with Loan Approval: Lenders rely on appraisals to approve loans, so this contingency is especially important if you're financing the purchase.

While waiving the appraisal contingency can make your offer more competitive, it can also expose you to financial risk if the home doesn't appraise for the agreed price.

How Contingencies Affect Your Offer

While contingencies are there to protect you, they can also make your offer less appealing to the seller, especially in a competitive market. Sellers prefer offers with fewer contingencies because they're more straightforward and less likely to fall through. However, this doesn't mean you should remove all contingencies just to win the home. You need to balance protecting yourself with making a strong offer.

Here are a few tips for managing contingencies:

Prioritize What's Most Important

Only include the contingencies you really need. For example, if you're confident about your financing but unsure about the home's condition, you might keep the inspection contingency but waive the financing one.

Be Flexible

Work with your real estate agent to find ways to make your offer competitive without giving up essential protections.

Shorten the Timeline

In some cases, you can make your offer more appealing by shortening the timeline for contingencies. For example, you could agree to complete the inspection within 7 days instead of the typical 10-14 days.

What Happens If Contingencies Aren't Met?

If a contingency isn't met, you have the right to cancel the deal without losing your earnest money. For example:

If the inspection reveals major problems and the seller won't fix them, you can walk away.

If your loan isn't approved, the financing contingency lets you back out.

If the home doesn't appraise for the agreed price, you can renegotiate or cancel the contract.

Without contingencies, you'd have to follow through with the purchase, even if unexpected problems arise.

Knowing When to Walk Away

Buying a home is a big decision, and while it's exciting, it's also important to stay alert for red flags that could turn your dream home into a nightmare. Sometimes, even when you find a house you love, the deal might not be worth it. Recognizing the signs that a home might not be the right choice can save you from regret and financial stress later. Here's how to spot red flags and know when it's time to walk away.

Issues Revealed During the Home Inspection

A home inspection is one of the most important steps in the buying process. It gives you a detailed report about the home's condition. While some issues are minor and can be fixed easily, others may be serious and costly to repair. Watch out for:

- Foundation Problems: Cracks in the foundation or uneven floors can indicate structural issues that are expensive to fix.
- Roof Damage: If the roof is old, leaky, or missing shingles, it could require a costly replacement.
- Water Damage or Mold: Stains on ceilings, walls, or floors may mean leaks. Mold can also cause health problems and may require professional removal.
- Electrical and Plumbing Issues: Outdated wiring or leaky pipes could lead to expensive repairs and safety concerns.

If the inspection reveals major problems and the seller isn't willing to fix them or lower the price, it may be a sign to walk away.

The Home Is Overpriced

When a home is priced higher than similar properties in the area, it's worth taking a closer look. Research the local market and compare prices for homes with similar features. If the home is overpriced and the seller won't negotiate, it may not be a wise investment.

Pay attention to the appraisal as well. If the home appraises for less than the agreed-upon price, your lender may not approve the full loan amount. In this case, you'd have to cover the difference out of pocket, which might not be worth it.

The Neighborhood Doesn't Fit Your Needs

The location of a home is just as important as the home itself. If the neighborhood doesn't meet your needs or feels unsafe, it's okay to walk away. Consider these factors:

Safety: Check crime rates and talk to neighbours to understand the area's safety.

Noise Levels: Visit the neighborhood at different times of the day to check for traffic, train noise, or other disturbances.

Amenities: Make sure the area has what you need, such as schools, grocery stores, parks, or public transportation.

Even the perfect house can feel wrong if the neighborhood isn't a good fit.

The Seller Is Unreasonable

Sellers who are unwilling to negotiate or work with you during the buying process can create unnecessary stress. For example, if the seller refuses to address issues found during the inspection or set unrealistic deadlines, it might be a sign of trouble. A cooperative seller makes the process smoother, while a difficult one can cause delays or problems.

Your Finances Don't Feel Right

It's easy to get caught up in the excitement of buying a home, but staying within your budget is crucial. If the cost of the home, including repairs or upgrades, stretches your finances too thin, it's better to walk away. Owning a home should bring stability, not financial stress.

Ask yourself:

- Will I still have enough money for other expenses and emergencies?
- Can I comfortably afford the monthly mortgage payments, taxes, and insurance?

If the answer is no, it's a sign to reconsider the purchase.

The Home Has Title Problems

The title of a home shows who legally owns it. Before you buy, a title company will check for any issues, like unpaid taxes or disputes over ownership. If there are problems with the title, it could delay the sale or even make it impossible to close the deal. If the title issues can't be resolved, walking away is the safest choice.

You Feel Pressured to Decide Quickly

Buying a home is a big decision that requires careful thought. If you feel rushed by the seller or your real estate agent to make a decision, it's a red flag. Take your time to evaluate the home, review the inspection report, and think about your long-term needs. Pressure to act quickly can lead to mistakes or regret.

Your Gut Tells You Something Is Off

Sometimes, you might not be able to pinpoint exactly what's wrong, but your instincts tell you something isn't right. Maybe the house feels too good to be true, or you notice small things that make you uneasy. Trust your instincts. If something doesn't feel right, it's okay to walk away and keep looking.

Unusual Restrictions or HOA Rules

If the home is part of a homeowner's association (HOA), review the rules and fees carefully. Some HOAs have strict regulations about what you can and can't do with your property, such as painting your house or parking in certain areas. If the rules feel too restrictive or the fees are too high, it may not be worth it.

The Home Requires Too Many Repairs

Fixer-uppers can be exciting, but they're not for everyone. If the home needs extensive repairs and you don't have the time, money, or skills to handle them, it's better to move on. Even if the price seems low, the cost of repairs can quickly add up, leaving you overwhelmed.

When to Walk Away

Walking away from a deal doesn't mean failure—it means you're protecting yourself from making a decision you might regret. Always prioritize your needs, budget, and long-term goals. A home is one of the biggest investments you'll make, so it's important to get it right.

10

Navigating Home Inspections and Appraisals

The Role of a Home Inspection

A home inspection is a key part of the home-buying process that helps you understand the condition of the house. It's not just a formality—it's a way to protect yourself from hidden problems and make sure the home is worth the price you're paying. Let's explore why home inspections are so important and what you can expect during the process.

Why Home Inspections Matter

A home inspection gives you a clear picture of the property's condition. While a home might look perfect on the outside, it could have hidden issues that aren't obvious during a quick walkthrough. An inspection helps uncover these problems, so you don't face unexpected repairs or costs after you move in.

Here are the main reasons why inspections are important:

Spotting Problems Early

Inspections reveal issues that could turn into bigger, more expensive problems later. For example, a small roof leak could lead to water damage or mold if not addressed.

Negotiating Repairs or Price

If the inspection finds problems, you can ask the seller to fix them or lower the price to cover the cost of repairs. This can save you a lot of money in the long run.

Understanding the Home's Condition

Knowing the home's condition helps you decide if it's worth buying. If the issues are too serious or expensive to fix, you can walk away before finalizing the deal.

Planning for Future Repairs

Even if the home is in good shape overall, the inspection report can help you plan for future maintenance. For example, the inspector might tell you that the water heater is old and will need replacing soon.

What Happens During a Home Inspection?

A home inspection is usually scheduled after your offer has been accepted but before the deal is finalized. The process typically takes 2–4 hours, depending on the size of the home. A licensed inspector will carefully examine the property and provide you with a detailed report of their findings.

Here's what to expect:

Exterior Inspection

The inspector will start by looking at the outside of the home. They'll check the condition of the roof, gutters, siding, and foundation. They'll also look for signs of water damage, cracks, or structural issues.

Interior Inspection

Inside the home, the inspector will examine the walls, floors, ceilings, and windows. They'll look for signs of damage, like cracks, stains, or uneven surfaces.

Plumbing

The inspector will test faucets, showers, and toilets to make sure they work properly. They'll also check for leaks, water pressure, and the condition of the water heater.

Electrical Systems

They'll test outlets, switches, and the circuit breaker to ensure everything is safe and up to code. Faulty wiring or outdated electrical systems can be a safety hazard.

Heating and Cooling Systems

The inspector will check the furnace, air conditioner, and ventilation systems to make sure they're functioning correctly.

Appliances

If appliances like the stove, refrigerator, or dishwasher are included in the sale, the inspector will test them to ensure they work.

Attic and Basement

The inspector will look for proper insulation and ventilation in the attic and check the basement for signs of moisture, mold, or foundation problems.

What's Not Included in a Home Inspection

It's important to know that a home inspection doesn't cover everything. For example, the inspector won't check for pests, like termites, unless you hire a specialist. They also won't inspect parts of the home they can't easily access, like underground pipes or hidden wiring. If you're concerned about these areas, you may need additional inspections.

Who Should Attend the Inspection?

As the buyer, it's a good idea to attend the home inspection if possible. This gives you a chance to ask questions and see any issues firsthand. Your real estate agent might also attend to help you understand the findings and discuss next steps. The seller doesn't usually attend, but their agent might.

What Happens After the Inspection?

Once the inspection is complete, the inspector will provide you with a detailed report. This report includes:

I. A summary of the home's overall condition.
II. A list of issues found during the inspection.
III. Photos and descriptions of specific problems.
IV. Recommendations for repairs or further evaluations.

After reviewing the report, you'll have a few options:

Ask the Seller for Repairs

If the inspection reveals significant issues, you can ask the seller to fix them before closing. For example, if the roof needs repairs, the seller might agree to cover the cost.

Negotiate the Price

Instead of asking for repairs, you can request a lower price to cover the cost of fixing the issues yourself.

Accept the Home as Is

If the problems are minor or you're comfortable handling the repairs, you can move forward without asking for changes.

Walk Away

If the issues are too serious and the seller isn't willing to address them, you can cancel the deal. This is why having an inspection contingency in your offer is so important.

How to Choose a Good Home Inspector

A thorough inspection depends on having a qualified and experienced inspector. Here are some tips for choosing the right one:

I. Check Credentials: Make sure the inspector is licensed and certified in your state.

II. Read Reviews: Look for online reviews or ask friends and family for recommendations.

III. Ask About Experience: An inspector with years of experience is more likely to spot hidden issues.

IV. Review a Sample Report: Ask to see a sample inspection report to make sure it's clear and detailed.

Key Areas Inspected During a Home Inspection

A home inspection is a detailed review of the property's condition. The inspector looks for problems in key areas of the home, such as the roof, foundation, HVAC system, plumbing, and electrical systems. Knowing what's inspected and why can help you understand the process better.

Roofing

The roof is one of the most important parts of a home because it protects everything underneath it. If the roof is damaged, it can lead to leaks, water damage, and even structural problems. During the inspection, the inspector will check:

- Shingles and Tiles: Are they missing, cracked, or curling? Damaged shingles can allow water to seep in.
- Flashing: This is the material around chimneys, vents, and skylights that prevents leaks. The inspector will ensure it's in good condition.
- Gutters and Downspouts: These help direct water away from the home. Clogged or damaged gutters can cause water to pool near the foundation.
- Signs of Leaks: Inside the home, the inspector will look for water stains on ceilings and walls, which could indicate a roof problem.

If the roof is old or in poor condition, the inspector may recommend repairs or replacement. Knowing the roof's condition helps you plan for future costs.

Foundation

The foundation supports the entire home, so any issues here can be serious. Problems with the foundation can cause walls to crack, doors to stick, and floors to become uneven. The inspector will look for:

- Cracks: Small cracks are often normal, but large or uneven cracks could mean structural problems.
- Shifting or Settling: If the foundation has moved or settled, it can affect the stability of the home.
- Water Damage: Moisture near the foundation can weaken it over time. The inspector will check for signs of water pooling or drainage issues.

A strong foundation is essential for a safe and stable home. If there are foundation problems, they can be expensive to fix, so it's important to identify them early.

HVAC System

The HVAC (heating, ventilation, and air conditioning) system keeps the home comfortable year-round. During the inspection, the inspector will check:

- Furnace and Air Conditioner: Are they working properly? The inspector will test the systems and look for signs of wear and tear.
- Age of the System: Most HVAC systems last 15–20 years. If the system is old, you may need to replace it soon.
- Air Filters and Ductwork: Clean filters and ducts are important for good airflow and indoor air quality.

A well-maintained HVAC system is essential for comfort and energy efficiency. If the system needs repairs or replacement, it's good to know before buying the home.

Plumbing

The plumbing system delivers water to the home and removes waste. The inspector will examine:

- Pipes and Fixtures: Are there leaks, corrosion, or damage? Leaks can cause water damage and mold.
- Water Pressure: Low water pressure might indicate a problem with the pipes.
- Water Heater: The inspector will check the water heater's condition, age, and capacity to ensure it meets the needs of the household.
- Sewage and Drainage: The inspector will check for clogs or signs of slow drainage in sinks, showers, and toilets.

Plumbing problems can be costly to fix, so it's important to know the condition of the system before finalizing the purchase.

Electrical Systems

The electrical system powers the home, so it's important for it to be safe and up to code. The inspector will look at:

- Wiring: Are the wires outdated or damaged? Faulty wiring can be a fire hazard.
- Outlets and Switches: Do they work properly? The inspector will check for GFCI outlets in areas like kitchens and bathrooms for added safety.
- Breaker Panel: The inspector will ensure the circuit breaker is properly labelled and can handle the home's electrical needs.

Electrical repairs can be dangerous and expensive, so it's essential to address any issues before closing the deal.

Appraisal Basics: Why They Matter

An appraisal is different from a home inspection. While the inspection focuses on the home's condition, the appraisal determines its market value. Lenders require an appraisal to ensure the home is worth the amount they're lending you. This step protects both you and the lender from overpaying for a property.

1. How Appraisals Work

During an appraisal, a licensed appraiser visits the property to assess its value. They consider factors such as:

Size and Layout

How big is the home, and how is it designed?

Condition

Is the home well-maintained, or does it need repairs?

Comparable Sales

The appraiser looks at recent sales of similar homes in the area to determine what the property is worth.

Location

Homes in desirable neighbourhoods tend to have higher values.

After the visit, the appraiser provides a report with the home's appraised value.

2. Why Appraisals Are Important

Appraisals play a crucial role in the home-buying process for several reasons:

Protecting Your Investment

The appraisal ensures you're not paying more than the home is worth.

Loan Approval

Lenders use the appraised value to determine how much they'll lend you. If the appraisal is lower than the purchase price, you may need to renegotiate with the seller or cover the difference out of pocket.

Peace of Mind

Knowing the home's value helps you feel confident in your purchase.

3. What Happens If the Appraisal Is Low

If the appraised value is lower than the agreed price, there are a few options:

Negotiate with the Seller

Ask the seller to lower the price to match the appraisal.

Pay the Difference

If you can afford it, you can cover the gap between the appraised value and the purchase price.

Walk Away

If you included an appraisal contingency in your offer, you can cancel the deal without losing your earnest money.

A low appraisal doesn't have to ruin the deal, but it's important to know your options.

What to Do if Issues Arise

A home inspection can reveal problems with the property that you might not have noticed before. While some issues may be minor, others can be costly to fix. If the inspection uncovers problems, don't panic. Instead, you can use this information to negotiate with the seller. Here's how to handle the situation and come to a fair agreement.

Review the Inspection Report Carefully

After the inspection, you'll receive a detailed report outlining the home's condition. Take time to review it thoroughly, focusing on major issues like roofing problems, structural damage, plumbing leaks, or electrical hazards. Minor repairs, such as a squeaky door or chipped paint, are usually not worth negotiating unless they're part of a bigger problem.

Ask your real estate agent or the inspector to explain any technical terms or issues you don't understand. This will help you decide which problems are worth addressing.

Prioritize the Most Serious Issues

Not every problem needs to be fixed by the seller. Focus on big-ticket items that affect the home's safety, liveability, or value. These might include:

- A leaking roof or damaged shingles.
- Faulty wiring or outdated electrical systems.
- Plumbing issues like leaks or low water pressure.
- Structural problems such as foundation cracks.
- Mold, water damage, or pest infestations.

Cosmetic issues, like outdated fixtures or wall colours, are typically not part of the negotiation unless they were misrepresented in the listing.

Decide What You Want to Ask For

Once you've identified the major issues, decide how you'd like the seller to address them. You have a few options:

Request Repairs

Ask the seller to fix the problems before closing. This works well if the issues are straightforward and can be completed quickly.

Ask for a Credit

Instead of repairs, request a credit at closing. This means the seller gives you money to cover the cost of repairs, allowing you to handle them after you move in.

Negotiate a Price Reduction

If the repairs are extensive, you can ask the seller to lower the home's price. This option gives you flexibility to manage the repairs yourself.

Discuss these options with your real estate agent to determine the best approach.

Write a Repair Request

A repair request is a formal document that outlines the issues you want addressed and how you'd like the seller to handle them. Be specific about what you're asking for. For example:

- Instead of saying, "Fix the plumbing," specify, "Repair the leak under the kitchen sink."
- Instead of "Repair the roof," specify, "Replace missing shingles on the roof."

A clear and professional repair request increases the chances of reaching an agreement with the seller.

Negotiate with the Seller

Once the repair request is submitted, the seller may respond in a few ways:

- Agree to All Requests: The seller might agree to fix the issues, provide a credit, or reduce the price as you requested.
- Offer a Compromise: The seller might agree to some of your requests but decline others. For example, they might fix the roof but refuse to repair minor plumbing issues.

- Refuse to Address Any Issues: In rare cases, the seller may refuse to negotiate.

Be prepared to compromise. The goal is to find a solution that works for both you and the seller.

Know When to Walk Away

If the seller refuses to address serious issues and you're not comfortable moving forward, it's okay to walk away. This is why having an inspection contingency in your offer is so important—it allows you to back out of the deal without losing your earnest money. Sometimes, walking away is the best decision if the home's problems are too costly or risky.

Plan for Repairs After Closing

If the seller agrees to provide a credit or reduce the price, you'll handle the repairs yourself after closing. Make sure to get quotes from professionals so you know how much the repairs will cost. Budget for these expenses, and prioritize the most urgent repairs first.

11

Closing the Deal

Understanding Closing Costs

Closing costs are an important part of buying a home. These are the fees and expenses you pay when the sale of the house is finalized, often referred to as "closing." Many first-time buyers don't realize how many costs are involved, so it's helpful to understand what to expect. Closing costs can vary based on where you live, the price of the home, and your loan type, but they usually range from 2% to 5% of the home's purchase price. Let's break down the typical fees so you know where your money goes.

Loan Origination Fee

The loan origination fee is paid to your lender for processing your mortgage. It's typically 0.5% to 1% of the loan amount. This fee covers the lender's administrative costs, such as reviewing your application, verifying your credit, and creating the loan documents.

For example, if your loan is $200,000, the loan origination fee might be around $2,000. It's a standard part of most mortgages, so be prepared for this cost.

Title Insurance

Title insurance protects both you and your lender from any legal issues related to the ownership of the property. Before closing, a title company will check the property's history to make sure there are no disputes over ownership, unpaid taxes, or other claims. If a problem arises later, title insurance ensures you're not financially responsible.

There are two types of title insurance:

I. Owner's Title Insurance: Protects you as the buyer.

II. Lender's Title Insurance: Protects the lender's interest in the property.

The cost of title insurance varies but is usually a one-time fee based on the price of the home.

Escrow Fees

Escrow is a neutral third party that holds money and important documents during the closing process. The escrow company ensures that all conditions of the sale are met before the funds are released to the seller. For example, they'll make sure the down payment, loan, and other fees are paid correctly.

Escrow fees are typically split between the buyer and the seller. The exact amount depends on your location and the company handling the escrow, but it's usually around 1% of the home's purchase price.

Appraisal Fee

An appraisal fee covers the cost of determining the value of the home. Your lender requires an appraisal to make sure the property is worth the amount they're lending you. A licensed appraiser visits the home, examines its condition, and compares it to similar homes in the area to come up with a value.

The appraisal fee is usually between $300 and $500, depending on the size and location of the home.

Home Inspection Fee

While not always included in the official closing costs, many buyers choose to pay for a home inspection before finalizing the deal. A home inspection ensures there are no hidden problems with the property, such as plumbing leaks or electrical issues.

Home inspection fees typically range from $300 to $600. This is a small price to pay for peace of mind and to avoid costly surprises later.

Property Taxes

At closing, you'll need to pay property taxes for the portion of the year you'll own the home. For example, if the seller has already paid property taxes for the entire year, you'll reimburse them for your share starting from the day you take ownership.

The amount of property taxes varies based on your location and the value of the home. Your lender will usually calculate this amount and include it in your closing costs.

Private Mortgage Insurance (PMI)

If your down payment is less than 20% of the home's purchase price, your lender may require private mortgage insurance (PMI). This protects the lender in case you stop making payments on the loan. PMI is often paid monthly, but some lenders require you to pay a portion upfront at closing.

The upfront PMI fee is usually 1% of the loan amount. For example, on a $200,000 loan, the PMI fee could be $2,000.

Recording Fees

Recording fees are paid to your local government to officially register the sale of the home. This makes the transaction a public record and ensures that the property's ownership is updated with your name.

The cost of recording fees is usually between $100 and $250, depending on your location.

Attorney Fees

In some states, it's required to have an attorney present at closing to review the documents and ensure everything is legally binding. Even if it's not required, some buyers choose to hire an attorney for added protection.

Attorney fees vary widely but can range from $500 to $1,500.

Prepaid Costs

Prepaid costs are expenses that you pay in advance at closing. These include:

- Homeowner's Insurance: Your lender requires you to have insurance in place to protect the property. You'll typically pay the first year's premium upfront.
- Interest: If your loan closes in the middle of the month, you'll pay interest from the closing date to the end of the month.

These costs can add up, so make sure to budget for them.

Miscellaneous Fees

There may be other small fees included in your closing costs, such as:

- Courier Fees: For delivering documents.
- Notary Fees: For verifying signatures on legal documents.
- Flood Certification Fee: To determine if the home is in a flood zone and requires special insurance.

While these fees are usually small, they can add to the total amount you'll need to pay.

How to Prepare for Closing Costs

To avoid surprises, ask your lender for a Loan Estimate early in the process. This document outlines the estimated closing costs so you can budget accordingly. A few days before closing, you'll receive a Closing Disclosure that shows the final costs. Review it carefully and ask your real estate agent or lender if you have any questions.

Final Walkthrough Checklist

The final walkthrough is one of the last steps before you officially buy your home. It's your chance to make sure everything is in order and the property is in the condition you agreed upon. This walkthrough usually happens a day or two before closing. While it's an exciting moment, it's important to stay focused and check everything carefully. Here's a simple checklist to help you during your final walkthrough.

Confirm Repairs Have Been Completed

If you negotiated repairs with the seller based on the home inspection, the final walkthrough is your chance to confirm that they've been completed. Bring a copy of the inspection report and the repair agreement so you can double-check the items on the list.

- Look at the areas that needed fixing, such as plumbing, electrical systems, or roofing.
- Ask for receipts or proof of completed repairs if the seller hasn't already provided them.

If the repairs haven't been done or are not up to standard, let your real estate agent know immediately.

Check for Damage or Changes

During the walkthrough, make sure the property hasn't been damaged or changed since your last visit. Sometimes, moving furniture or appliances can leave behind scratches, dents, or other issues.

- Look at walls, floors, and ceilings for new stains, cracks, or holes.
- Check for broken windows or doors that weren't damaged before.
- Walk around the yard to ensure the landscaping is in the same condition as when you made your offer.

If you notice any new problems, bring them to the seller's attention before closing.

Test All Appliances

If the home comes with appliances, like a stove, refrigerator, washer, or dryer, make sure they are in working order.

- Turn on the stove and oven to ensure they heat up properly.
- Check that the refrigerator and freezer are cold.

- Run the dishwasher, washer, and dryer briefly to confirm they work.

If any appliances aren't functioning, you may need to negotiate with the seller to fix or replace them.

Inspect the Plumbing

It's important to make sure the plumbing is in good condition during the final walkthrough. Here's what to check:

- Turn on all faucets and showers to ensure there's good water pressure and hot water.
- Flush all toilets to confirm they work properly.
- Look under sinks for leaks or drips.
- Check outdoor faucets to ensure they work as well.

If you find plumbing issues, notify your agent so they can address it with the seller.

Test Electrical Systems

Test the home's electrical systems to ensure everything is working as it should.

- Turn on all light switches and ensure the lights work.
- Test outlets by plugging in a phone charger or small device.
- Check ceiling fans to make sure they operate correctly.
- Test any built-in systems, like doorbells, garage door openers, or security systems.

If you find any issues, make a note of them and let your agent know.

Open and Close Windows and Doors

Windows and doors should open, close, and lock properly. During the walkthrough:

- Open and close every door, including closet doors, to ensure they don't stick or make noise.

- Test all window locks and make sure the windows open and shut easily.
- Check for drafts or broken seals on windows.

Secure doors and windows are essential for safety and comfort.

Verify Items Included in the Sale

Make sure all items that were part of the sale are still in the home. These might include light fixtures, curtains, or outdoor equipment like a shed or swing set. Walk through the home with the purchase agreement to confirm that everything listed is present and accounted for.

Check the Heating and Cooling Systems

Turn on the heating and cooling systems to make sure they work properly. This is especially important if the weather has changed since your initial inspection. If the home has a thermostat, make sure it's functioning and can control the temperature as expected.

Look for Signs of Pests

During the walkthrough, check for signs of pests like rodents or insects. Look for droppings, chewed wires, or holes in walls and cabinets. If you notice signs of pests, you may need to discuss treatment with the seller before closing.

Test the Water Heater

Make sure the water heater is providing hot water and doesn't show signs of damage or leaks. Turn on a few faucets and showers to ensure the hot water is consistent and doesn't run out too quickly.

Walk Around the Exterior

Inspect the exterior of the home to ensure everything is in the condition you expect. Look at the roof, gutters, siding, and foundation for any damage or changes. Check the garage or storage areas as well, and confirm that any outdoor fixtures or equipment are still there.

Bring a Checklist and Take Notes

To stay organized, bring this checklist with you and take notes during the walkthrough. Write down anything that seems off or needs attention. Your real estate agent can help you address any concerns with the seller before closing.

Reviewing Closing Documents

When buying a home, closing day is when you sign the documents that make the house officially yours. While this is an exciting moment, it's also important to carefully review the key documents to ensure everything is correct. These papers include the deed, loan agreement, disclosures, and title. Let's break down what each document means and why it's important to review them.

The Deed

The deed is the document that transfers ownership of the home from the seller to you. It's one of the most important papers in the closing process. Once signed, it becomes a legal record showing that you are the new owner of the property.

What to Check:

- Make sure your name is spelled correctly.
- Confirm the property's address and legal description are accurate.
- Verify that the seller's name matches the previous ownership records.

The deed will be recorded with your local government to make the transfer of ownership official. If there are any mistakes, they could cause problems later, so review this document carefully.

The Loan Agreement

The loan agreement is the contract between you and your lender. It outlines the terms of your mortgage, including how much you're borrowing, the interest rate, and the repayment schedule. This document is critical because it explains your financial responsibilities over the life of the loan.

What to Check:

- Confirm the loan amount matches what you agreed to borrow.
- Double-check the interest rate to ensure it's correct.
- Review the loan term (e.g., 15 or 30 years) and monthly payment amount.
- Look for any fees or penalties, such as late payment charges or prepayment penalties.

Understanding your loan agreement helps you avoid surprises and ensures you're comfortable with the terms of your mortgage.

Closing Disclosure

The closing disclosure is a detailed summary of all the costs involved in buying the home. Your lender must provide this document at least three days before closing so you have time to review it. The closing disclosure shows your loan terms, monthly payments, and a breakdown of closing costs.

What to Check:

- Compare the loan terms and costs with the estimate you received earlier.
- Make sure the closing costs match what you expected to pay.
- Confirm the total amount you need to bring to closing, including your down payment and fees.

If you notice any differences between the closing disclosure and earlier estimates, ask your lender or real estate agent to explain the changes before signing.

Title Documents

The title documents show that the seller has the legal right to sell the home and that there are no outstanding claims or disputes on the property. These papers also include title insurance, which protects you and your lender from any future issues related to the property's ownership.

What to Check:

- Ensure the title is "clear," meaning there are no liens, unpaid taxes, or legal claims against the property.
- Review the title insurance policy to understand what it covers.

Having a clear title ensures you won't face legal challenges to your ownership in the future.

Affidavit of Title

This document is provided by the seller and confirms that they are the legal owner of the property. It also states that there are no new legal issues, such as liens or disputes, that could affect the sale.

What to Check:

- Verify the seller's information matches what's in the other documents.
- Confirm there are no recent changes that could affect the sale.

The affidavit of title gives you added confidence that the transaction is legitimate and problem-free.

Bill of Sale

If the sale includes items like appliances, fixtures, or furniture, the bill of sale lists these items. It ensures that everything you agreed to buy with the home is included.

What to Check:

- Confirm the items listed match what you agreed to in the purchase agreement.
- Make sure the document is signed by the seller.

The bill of sale protects you in case the seller removes any agreed-upon items before you take possession of the home.

Mortgage Note

The mortgage note is a document you sign to promise repayment of the loan. It's like an IOU to the lender and includes details about your monthly payments, interest rate, and loan term.

What to Check:

- Confirm the loan amount, interest rate, and term match the loan agreement.
- Review the payment schedule and due dates.

By signing the mortgage note, you're agreeing to repay the lender under the terms listed, so it's important to make sure everything is accurate.

Escrow Statement

If your lender is setting up an escrow account to pay property taxes and homeowner's insurance, the escrow statement will outline how much money is being collected and how it will be used.

What to Check:

- Verify that the estimated amounts for taxes and insurance are correct.
- Confirm the escrow account balance matches what you've paid so far.

The escrow statement helps you understand how much money is being held and ensures there are no unexpected charges.

Certificate of Occupancy (If Applicable)

In some cases, you may need a certificate of occupancy to confirm the home is safe and meets local building codes. This is more common with new construction or recently renovated homes.

What to Check:

- Ensure the certificate is included if it's required in your area.
- Verify that it's issued by the proper local authority.

Having this document ensures the home is ready for you to move in.

How to Review Your Documents

Reviewing all these documents can feel overwhelming, but taking the time to do it thoroughly is worth it. Here are some tips to make the process easier:

- Ask Questions: If there's anything you don't understand, ask your real estate agent, attorney, or lender for clarification.
- Take Your Time: Don't feel rushed. Make sure you have enough time to read and understand everything before signing.
- Double-Check Details: Look for typos, errors, or incorrect amounts. Even small mistakes can cause problems later.

Funding Your Closing

Closing day is when all the hard work of buying a home finally pays off, and the property officially becomes yours. However, before you can get the keys to your new home, you'll need to prepare your funds to cover the closing costs. These include fees, taxes, and your down payment. Getting your finances ready in advance will make the process smooth and stress-free. Here's a step-by-step guide to help you prepare your funds and payment methods for closing day.

1. Know the Total Amount Needed

The first step is understanding exactly how much money you need to bring to closing. Your lender will give you a document called the Closing Disclosure a few days before closing day. This document lists all the costs you'll need to pay, including:

Down Payment

This is the portion of the home's purchase price that you pay upfront. It's usually a percentage of the total price, such as 3%, 10%, or 20%.

Closing Costs

These are the fees for services like the loan, title search, and home inspection. They typically range from 2% to 5% of the home's purchase price.

Prepaid Costs

These include property taxes and homeowner's insurance that you pay in advance.

Review the Closing Disclosure carefully and confirm the total amount needed with your lender or real estate agent.

2. Decide on the Payment Method

Most closing agents require funds to be paid in a secure and traceable way. Personal checks or cash are usually not accepted. Here are the two most common payment methods:

Wire Transfer

You can send the funds electronically from your bank to the escrow or closing agent. This is a fast and secure method. However, you'll need to coordinate with your bank and confirm the wire transfer details with the closing agent. Be cautious of wire transfer scams—always double-check the account information.

Cashier's Check

This is a check issued by your bank, guaranteed to have the funds available. You'll need to visit your bank in person to request the check and bring it with you to the closing.

Ask your closing agent which payment method they prefer and plan accordingly.

3. Arrange Your Funds Ahead of Time

Once you know the total amount and payment method, it's time to ensure the money is ready. Follow these steps to organize your funds:

Transfer Money to the Right Account

If your savings and checking accounts are separate, transfer the necessary funds to the account you'll use for the payment.

Check Daily Limits

Some banks have daily limits on wire transfers or cashier's checks. Make sure your limit is high enough to cover the closing costs. If not, contact your bank to request an increase.

Request Funds in Advance

If you're using a cashier's check, visit your bank a day or two before closing to get the check. This ensures you're not rushing on closing day.

4. Verify Payment Details

Before sending a wire, transfer or requesting a cashier's check, verify the payment details with your closing agent. Double-check the following:

Account Information

If you're wiring funds, confirm the account number and routing number with the closing agent.

Payee Name

Ensure the cashier's check is made out to the correct payee, such as the title company or escrow agent.

Exact Amount

Verify the total amount you need to pay to avoid any discrepancies.

5. Plan for Extra Costs

It's a good idea to have a little extra money in your account for unexpected costs. For example, there might be last-minute adjustments to property taxes or other fees. Having a financial cushion can save you from any surprises.

6. Bring Identification

On closing day, you'll need to bring a valid photo ID, such as a driver's license or passport. The closing agent will use this to confirm your identity before finalizing the transaction. Make sure your ID is current and matches the name on the closing documents.

7. Stay in Contact with Your Team

If you have any questions or concerns about the payment process, reach out to your real estate agent, lender, or closing agent. They're there to help you and can provide guidance if anything is unclear.

8. What Happens If You Don't Have the Funds Ready?

Not having the funds ready on closing day can delay the process or even cause the deal to fall through. To avoid this, double-check everything in advance and make sure you've followed all the steps above. If there's an issue with your bank or payment method, let your closing agent know immediately so they can work with you to resolve it.

12

Moving into Your New Home

Preparing for the Move

Moving into your new home is an exciting moment, but it can also feel overwhelming. There are so many things to do, from packing your belongings to arranging transportation. The key to a smooth move is preparation. By planning ahead, staying organized, and knowing what to expect, you can make the process much easier. Here's a simple guide with tips on packing, choosing a moving company, and creating a checklist.

1. Start with a Moving Checklist

A checklist is your best friend during a move. It helps you keep track of everything you need to do and ensures you don't forget anything important. Here's how to create one:

- List Tasks by Priority: Write down everything you need to do, such as packing, cancelling utilities at your old home, and setting up services at your new home.
- Set Deadlines: Assign deadlines to each task. For example, aim to pack certain rooms by specific dates.
- Include Small Details: Don't forget smaller tasks like changing your address with the post office or notifying your bank.

Keeping your checklist handy will make the moving process feel more manageable.

2. Packing Tips for a Stress-Free Move

Packing is one of the most time-consuming parts of moving. Start early and follow these tips to make it easier:

- Sort and Declutter: Before you pack, go through your belongings and decide what to keep, donate, or throw away. Moving is a great opportunity to get rid of things you no longer need.
- Pack by Room: Pack items from one room at a time. This makes unpacking at your new home much easier.
- Label Boxes Clearly: Write the name of the room and a brief description of what's inside on each box. For example, "Kitchen - Plates and Glasses." This helps you find things quickly.
- Use Quality Packing Supplies: Invest in sturdy boxes, packing tape, and bubble wrap to protect your items. For fragile items, like dishes or glassware, wrap them in newspaper or bubble wrap.
- Pack an Essentials Box: Put together a box with items you'll need right away, such as toiletries, a change of clothes, important documents, and chargers. Keep this box with you during the move.

3. Choosing a Moving Company

If you're hiring professional movers, take the time to choose a reliable company. Here's what to look for:

- Get Recommendations: Ask friends, family, or your real estate agent for recommendations. You can also read online reviews to see what others have experienced.
- Request Quotes: Contact multiple moving companies to get quotes. Make sure the quotes include all costs, such as packing, transportation, and unloading.
- Check for Licenses and Insurance: Make sure the company is licensed and has insurance to protect your belongings in case of damage.
- Ask Questions: Find out if the movers will handle special items, like heavy furniture or fragile valuables.

If you're moving on your own, rent a moving truck early to avoid last-minute stress.

4. Organize Utilities and Services

Before moving day, arrange for utilities and services at your new home. Here's what to do:

- Set Up Utilities: Contact the utility companies to arrange for water, electricity, gas, and internet to be turned on before you move in.
- Cancel Old Services: Notify the utility providers at your old home about your moving date so they can stop services.
- Forward Your Mail: Change your address with the post office so your mail gets forwarded to your new home.

Handling these tasks ahead of time ensures you'll have everything ready when you arrive.

5. Plan Moving Day Details

On moving day, things can feel hectic, but staying organized will help. Here's how to plan for the big day:

- Confirm Arrangements: Double-check the schedule with your moving company or friends who are helping you.
- Keep Important Items with You: Carry valuables like jewellery, important documents, and electronics with you instead of packing them with other items.
- Stay Hydrated and Take Breaks: Moving can be tiring, so remember to drink water and rest when needed.

If you're moving with children or pets, make plans to keep them safe and comfortable during the move.

6. Unpacking and Settling In

Once you arrive at your new home, start by unpacking the essentials box. This will give you access to the items you need right away. Then, unpack room by room, starting with the kitchen, bathroom, and bedrooms.

As you settle in, take your time arranging furniture and organizing your belongings. Moving into a new home is a fresh start, so enjoy making the space your own.

Setting Up Utilities and Services

Moving into a new home is exciting, but before you can fully enjoy it, you need to make sure all the essential services are set up. These include utilities like water, electricity, gas, and internet, which are necessary for comfort and convenience. Getting everything arranged in advance will ensure your home is ready to use from day one. Here's a step-by-step guide to help you set up utilities and services.

1. Create a List of Essential Utilities

Before you start, make a list of the utilities and services you'll need in your new home. These typically include:

- Electricity: Keeps your lights and appliances running.
- Water and Sewer: Supplies clean water and manages waste.
- Gas (if applicable): Powers stoves, heaters, and water heaters in many homes.
- Trash and Recycling: Ensures garbage and recyclables are collected regularly.
- Internet and Phone Services: Keeps you connected online and by phone.

Knowing what you need will help you stay organized as you contact providers.

2. Research Providers in Your Area

Utility providers vary by location, so it's important to find out which companies service your new home. Here's how:

- Ask Your Real Estate Agent or Landlord: They often have information about local providers.
- Check Online: Most utility companies have websites where you can see if they serve your area.
- Ask Neighbours: If possible, ask your new neighbours for recommendations or advice on reliable providers.

Once you know which companies are available, compare their rates and services to choose the best options for your needs.

3. Contact Utility Companies Early

It's a good idea to contact utility companies at least two weeks before your move-in date. This gives them enough time to set up services and ensures there are no delays. Here's what to do:

- Electricity and Gas: Call the provider and give them your move-in date. They may need to schedule a time to turn on the service, especially for gas.
- Water and Sewer: Contact the local water company to set up an account. In some cases, these services are handled by the city, so you may need to call your local government office.
- Trash and Recycling: Ask the city or a private company about trash collection days and how to set up service.

Be ready to provide your new address and personal information, such as your name, phone number, and possibly a form of ID.

4. Arrange for Internet and Phone Services

Internet and phone services are just as important as utilities, especially if you work from home or need to stay connected with family and friends. Here's how to set them up:

- Choose a Provider: Research internet providers in your area. Compare their plans, speeds, and prices to find the best fit for your needs.

- Schedule Installation: Some providers can activate internet service remotely, but others may need to send a technician to your home. Schedule the installation for a convenient time, ideally before or shortly after your move-in date.
- Check for Bundled Packages: Many companies offer discounts if you bundle internet, phone, and TV services together.

If you rely on mobile data for internet access, make sure your cell service is strong in the area.

5. Set Up Automatic Payments

To avoid missing payments, consider setting up automatic payments for your utilities and services. Most providers offer this option, allowing you to link your bank account or credit card. Automatic payments ensure your bills are paid on time and save you the hassle of remembering due dates.

6. Transfer or Cancel Old Services

If you're moving from another home, don't forget to cancel or transfer the utilities and services at your old address. Contact each provider and let them know your move-out date. Ask for a final bill to settle any outstanding charges.

For internet or cable services, return any rented equipment, such as modems or routers, to avoid additional fees. If you're transferring these services to your new home, confirm the transfer date to ensure uninterrupted service.

7. Keep Track of Utility Start Dates

As you set up utilities, make a note of when each service will start. This helps you keep track of everything and ensures all services are ready when you move in. For example:

- Electricity and water should be activated by your move-in day.

- Internet installation may take a few days, depending on the provider's availability.
- If you're unsure about start dates, confirm them with the providers.

8. Test Services After Moving In

Once you've moved into your new home, test each utility and service to make sure they're working properly:

- Electricity: Check lights, outlets, and appliances.
- Water: Turn on faucets and flush toilets to ensure there's running water.
- Gas: Test the stove or heating system if your home uses gas.
- Internet: Connect your devices to the network and test the speed.

If you notice any issues, contact the provider immediately for assistance.

9. Budget for Utility Costs

Utility bills can vary depending on the size of your home, the season, and your usage. To avoid surprises, ask the providers for an estimate of your monthly costs. Setting aside a portion of your budget for utilities ensures you're prepared for these expenses.

Making Your House a Home

A home is more than walls and furniture—it's a space that reflects your personality and feels comfortable, safe, and welcoming. Here are some simple tips to help you decorate, organize, and create a personal sanctuary in your new space.

Start with One Room at a Time

Moving in can feel overwhelming, so it's helpful to focus on one room at a time. Start with the spaces you'll use the most, such as the bedroom, kitchen, or living room. Once those areas feel settled, you can move on to other parts of the house.

1. Bedroom: This is where you rest and recharge, so make it cozy and inviting. Start with clean bedding, soft pillows, and your favourite colours.
2. Living Room: Add comfortable seating, such as a sofa or chairs, and decorate with personal touches like family photos or artwork.
3. Kitchen: Organize your essentials like utensils, pots, and dishes so you can start cooking meals right away.

By working room by room, you'll see progress and feel more at home faster.

Add Personal Touches

Adding personal items to your home makes it feel unique and special. These could include:

1. Photos: Display family photos on shelves, walls, or in a special gallery area.
2. Memories: Use keepsakes from travels or gifts from loved ones as part of your decor.
3. Artwork: Hang paintings, prints, or posters that reflect your style and interests.

These small touches will remind you of happy moments and make your space feel like it belongs to you.

Choose Colors That Make You Happy

Colors can affect how a room feels. Choose colors that make you feel relaxed, energized, or joyful, depending on the purpose of the space.

1. Soft Colors: Light blues, grays, or greens can create a calming atmosphere in bedrooms or bathrooms.
2. Bright Colors: Yellow, red, or orange can make kitchens or living rooms feel lively and cheerful.

3. Neutral Colors: Whites, tans, and beiges work well as a base, allowing you to add pops of color through decor like pillows or rugs.

If you're not ready to paint walls, try using colourful curtains, cushions, or throw blankets to add personality.

Organize Your Space

Good organization makes your home feel peaceful and functional. Start by organizing your belongings so everything has a place.

1. Declutter First: Before unpacking, get rid of items you don't need. This will save space and make organizing easier.
2. Use Storage Solutions: Use bins, baskets, or shelves to store items neatly. For example, use baskets for blankets or a rack for shoes by the door.
3. Label and Arrange: Labelling boxes or containers can help you find things quickly. Arrange items in a way that makes sense for how you'll use them.

An organized home is not only easier to maintain but also feels more welcoming.

Add Comfortable Textures

Textures play a big role in making your home cozy. Add layers of comfort with soft fabrics and materials:

1. Rugs: Place rugs in living areas or bedrooms to add warmth underfoot.
2. Throws and Pillows: Use plush throw blankets and pillows on your sofas or beds for a touch of softness.
3. Curtains: Hang curtains to soften windows and create privacy while adding style.

These small details make your home feel more comfortable and inviting.

Use Lighting to Set the Mood

Lighting can completely change how a room feels. Use a mix of lighting to make your home both functional and relaxing:

1. Overhead Lights: Brighten the entire room with ceiling lights for everyday use.
2. Lamps: Add floor or table lamps for soft, cozy lighting in the evenings.
3. Accent Lights: Use string lights, candles, or LED strips to add a touch of charm to specific areas.

Adjusting the lighting can create the right atmosphere for any time of day.

Create a Relaxation Space

Every home needs a spot where you can relax and recharge. This could be a reading nook, a cozy corner in your living room, or even a spot by the window with a comfortable chair.

1. Add a soft chair or cushion and a small table for books or a cup of tea.
2. Place plants nearby to add a sense of calm and connection to nature.
3. Make sure the space is quiet and away from distractions, so you can truly unwind.

Having a dedicated relaxation area helps you feel at ease in your home.

Add Plants for Life and Freshness

Plants can instantly make a house feel more alive. They add color, clean the air, and create a calming environment.

1. Small Plants: Place succulents or small potted plants on shelves, tables, or windowsills.
2. Larger Plants: Use tall plants, like a fiddle-leaf fig or snake plant, to fill empty corners.

3. Herbs: Grow herbs like basil or mint in the kitchen for a touch of green and fresh ingredients for cooking.

Caring for plants can also be a relaxing and rewarding part of making your house a home.

Meeting Your Neighbors and Engaging with the Community

Moving to a new neighborhood is exciting, but it can also feel a little unfamiliar at first. Meeting your neighbours and getting involved in the community is a great way to feel at home and build new connections. Here are some simple and friendly ideas to help you settle in and form relationships with the people around you.

Introduce Yourself

A friendly introduction goes a long way in making a good impression. When you see your neighbours outside, take a moment to say hello. It doesn't have to be a long conversation—a simple, "Hi, I just moved in next door," is enough to start.

- If you're feeling shy, try catching them while they're walking their dog or gardening. These are natural moments to begin a conversation.
- Share a little about yourself, like your name and what brought you to the area. You can also ask them about the neighborhood or recommend places to visit.

Attend Community Events

Local events are a great way to meet people and learn more about your neighborhood. Check for things like block parties, farmers' markets, or town festivals.

- Many neighbourhoods also host activities like movie nights in the park, garage sales, or food truck gatherings. These events provide a relaxed way to socialize.
- Joining a neighborhood group on social media or checking community boards at local coffee shops or libraries can help you stay updated on upcoming events.

Attending these activities helps you meet people who share your interests and gives you a chance to feel more connected to the area.

Bring a Small Gift

If you want to make a warm impression, consider giving your neighbours a small gift, such as cookies, a plant, or a handwritten note. This thoughtful gesture shows that you're friendly and happy to meet them.

- For example, you could say, "I wanted to drop these off to say hello. I'm excited to be part of the neighborhood!"
- If your neighbours welcome the gesture, it might lead to a longer conversation and a stronger connection.

Take Walks Around the Neighborhood

One of the easiest ways to meet neighbours is to spend time outdoors. Go for walks around your neighborhood, visit the local park, or sit on your front porch.

- You'll likely run into people walking their dogs, playing with their kids, or just enjoying the fresh air.
- A simple smile or wave can be a great way to start building relationships over time.

Walking around also helps you learn more about the community and feel more familiar with your surroundings.

Get Involved in Local Activities

Joining local groups or activities can help you meet people who share your interests. Consider:

- Volunteering: Look for opportunities to help at a food bank, animal shelter, or school event.
- Clubs or Classes: Join a book club, fitness class, or hobby group in your area.
- Religious or Cultural Groups: If you attend a church, mosque, temple, or other cultural group, this can be a wonderful way to connect with others.

These activities not only help you build friendships but also allow you to contribute to your community.

Be a Good Neighbour

Being kind and considerate makes it easier to form positive relationships. Show that you care about your neighborhood by:

1. Keeping your yard tidy and respecting shared spaces.
2. Offering help if a neighbour is carrying groceries or working on a project.
3. Being mindful of noise levels, especially in the evening.

Small acts of kindness can make a big difference in how your neighbours see you.

Host a Small Gathering

Once you feel comfortable, consider hosting a small gathering at your home or in your yard. It doesn't have to be fancy—something simple like coffee, tea, or snacks can work.

Hosting shows that you're interested in being part of the community and encourages others to reach out to you.

13

Managing Home Maintenance and Expenses

Home Maintenance Basics

Owning a home comes with responsibilities, and regular maintenance is one of the most important. Taking care of your home helps prevent costly repairs, keeps it safe, and ensures everything works properly. Here are some simple upkeep tips for key areas like the roof, plumbing, landscaping, and more to help new homeowners keep their homes in great shape.

Roof Maintenance

The roof protects your home from the elements, so keeping it in good condition is essential.

Inspect Regularly

Check your roof for loose or missing shingles, especially after storms. Look for any signs of damage, such as leaks or sagging areas.

Clean Gutters

Make sure gutters are free of leaves and debris so water can flow away from your home. Clogged gutters can lead to water damage.

Schedule Professional Inspections

Hire a professional to inspect your roof every few years to catch small issues before they become big problems.

Plumbing Care

Your plumbing system is key to running water and keeping your home functional. Simple maintenance can prevent leaks and water damage.

Check for Leaks

Regularly inspect faucets, pipes, and toilets for drips or leaks. Fixing small leaks early can save water and money.

Keep Drains Clear

Avoid pouring grease or food scraps down the sink. Use drain screens to catch hair and debris in bathrooms.

Test Water Pressure

If your water pressure is too high, it can damage pipes. A plumber can install a pressure regulator if needed.

Maintain the Water Heater

Flush the water heater once a year to remove sediment build up. This helps it run efficiently and last longer.

Landscaping and Yard Care

Taking care of your yard not only makes your home look nice but also prevents problems like pests and water damage.

Trim Trees and Bushes

Keep trees and bushes away from the house to prevent damage to siding or the roof. Overgrown branches can also attract pests.

Mow and Water the Lawn

Regular mowing keeps your lawn healthy, and watering during dry periods helps it stay green. Avoid overwatering to prevent soggy spots.

Inspect Sprinkler Systems

If you have a sprinkler system, check for leaks or broken heads to ensure it works properly.

HVAC Maintenance

Your heating, ventilation, and air conditioning (HVAC) system keeps your home comfortable year-round. Regular upkeep ensures it runs efficiently.

Change Filters

Replace air filters every 1–3 months to keep the system clean and improve air quality.

Schedule Service

Has your HVAC system professionally serviced once a year? This can help identify issues before they cause breakdowns.

Clean Vents

Vacuum air vents to remove dust and keep airflow steady.

Electrical System Checks

Keeping your electrical system in good condition is important for safety and preventing power outages.

Test Smoke Detectors

Check smoke and carbon monoxide detectors every few months. Replace batteries at least once a year.

Inspect Outlets and Cords

Look for frayed cords or loose outlets, and repair them immediately.

Label the Breaker Box

Make sure the circuit breakers are labelled correctly so you can quickly turn off power in an emergency.

General Maintenance Tips

There are other small tasks you can do regularly to keep your home in top shape.

Seal Windows and Doors

Check for drafts around windows and doors. Use weather stripping or caulk to seal gaps and save energy.

Clean Appliances

Keep your refrigerator coils clean and regularly clean your oven to ensure they work efficiently.

Check for Pests

Inspect your home for signs of pests like ants or rodents. If you notice an issue, address it quickly to prevent infestation.

Budgeting for Ongoing Expenses

Owning a home comes with responsibilities, including managing ongoing expenses. These costs include property taxes, utilities, and unexpected repairs. Planning for these expenses in advance can help you stay financially secure and avoid surprises. With a little organization, you can create a budget that ensures your home runs smoothly without stretching your finances.

Property taxes are one of the most important ongoing costs for homeowners. These taxes are determined by your local government and are based on the value of your home. Some lenders include property taxes in your monthly mortgage payments through an escrow account, which simplifies the process. However, if your taxes are not included, it's essential to plan for them. To do this, calculate the yearly tax amount and divide it into monthly savings. For instance, if your taxes are $3,600 annually, save $300 each month. Keep in mind that property taxes can increase if the value of your home rises or if local tax rates change. Reviewing your tax bill every year ensures you stay prepared for any adjustments.

Utilities are another significant ongoing expense. These include electricity, water, gas, internet, and trash collection—essential services that keep your home running. Utility costs depend on factors such as the size of your home, the number of people living there, and your usage habits. To estimate these costs, ask the utility companies or the previous homeowner for average monthly bills. Once you know the typical amounts, you can adjust your habits to save money, like turning off lights when not in use, fixing leaky faucets, or using energy-efficient appliances. Tracking your monthly bills will also help you spot patterns and identify areas where you can cut back.

Unexpected repairs are perhaps the most unpredictable part of homeownership. Even with proper maintenance, things like a leaky roof, a broken water heater, or a malfunctioning appliance can require immediate attention. To prepare for these surprises, create an emergency fund specifically for home repairs. A good rule of thumb is to save 1% of your home's value annually. For example, if your home is worth $250,000, aim to save $2,500 per year, or roughly $210 per month. Additionally, having a good homeowner's insurance policy can provide coverage for certain damages, such as those caused by storms or accidents. Regular maintenance of major systems like your roof, HVAC, and appliances can also extend their lifespans, reducing the chances of unexpected expenses.

Tracking your spending is essential for managing these costs effectively. Use a budgeting tool, whether it's a notebook, a spreadsheet, or a budgeting app, to record your monthly expenses. Review your spending at the end of each month to see how it compares to your budget. This practice helps you identify areas where you might be overspending and allows you to make adjustments. It's also a good idea to consider seasonal changes in your budget. For example, heating bills tend to rise in the winter, while cooling costs may increase during the summer. Saving extra money during lower-cost months can help cover these seasonal spikes.

Finally, take advantage of discounts and programs that can reduce your expenses. Many utility companies offer rebates for energy-efficient appliances or windows. Some even provide free energy audits to show you how to lower your energy usage. Additionally, check if your property taxes or home improvements qualify for tax deductions or credits. These small savings can add up and make a big difference over time.

Managing ongoing expenses like property taxes, utilities, and unexpected repairs is a key part of homeownership. By creating a budget, saving for emergencies, and keeping track of your spending, you can handle these costs with confidence. Planning ahead ensures that you're prepared for whatever comes your way, helping you enjoy the benefits of owning your home without unnecessary stress.

Building a Maintenance Schedule

Taking care of your home is much easier when you follow a maintenance schedule. This helps you stay organized, avoid problems, and keep your house in excellent condition. By dividing tasks into monthly, seasonal, and yearly plans, you can handle upkeep without stress. Here's how you can manage it step by step.

Monthly tasks involve small but important checks that ensure your home runs smoothly. For example, filters in your HVAC system should be inspected and cleaned or replaced each month. Clean filters improve air quality and help your heating and cooling systems work efficiently. Plumbing is another area to check regularly. Look under sinks and around appliances for leaks or drips. Fixing small leaks early prevents water damage and keeps your bills lower. Smoke and carbon monoxide detectors also need attention. Testing these devices monthly ensures they are working and keeps your home safe. Kitchen appliances like the stove, oven, and refrigerator should be wiped down frequently, and the fridge's coils can be cleaned to improve efficiency. Doors and windows should be inspected for drafts, and any cracks can be sealed with weather stripping or caulk to improve energy efficiency. Completing these small tasks each month helps avoid larger and more expensive issues in the future.

Seasonal maintenance prepares your home for changes in the weather and ensures it remains comfortable and safe. In spring, cleaning gutters and inspecting the roof for missing or damaged shingles are crucial steps. Gutters should be cleared of debris to prevent water damage, while roof checks help catch problems early. Spring is also a good time to service your air conditioning system so it is ready for the hotter months. Yard care, such as trimming bushes and reseeding the lawn, can make your outdoor space inviting. In summer, cleaning windows inside and out allows more natural light into your home. Sprinkler systems should be checked for leaks or blockages to maintain a healthy lawn. Decks and patios should also be inspected for loose boards or cracks that might need repair.

Fall brings cooler weather, making it essential to seal gaps and cracks around windows and doors to keep the heat inside. Gutters need to be cleaned again to prepare for winter and prevent ice build up. It's also the perfect time to service your furnace to ensure it works efficiently during colder months. As winter sets in, keeping an eye on snow and ice build up is vital for safety. Walkways and driveways should be cleared regularly to prevent accidents. Exposed pipes may need to be insulated, and cabinets should be kept open during freezing weather to avoid burst pipes. Checking insulation in attics and basements ensures your home stays warm while reducing energy bills.

Annual maintenance tasks focus on deeper inspections and upkeep that keep your home safe and functional in the long run. For instance, chimneys and fireplaces should be professionally cleaned to remove build up that could become a fire hazard. Draining your water heater once a year helps remove sediment, improving efficiency and extending its lifespan. Foundations should also be inspected for cracks or signs of movement to ensure the stability of your home. Professional carpet cleaning removes dirt and allergens, keeping your home fresh and clean. Major systems like the roof, plumbing, and HVAC should also be inspected by professionals once a year. These checks can catch small problems before they become costly repairs.

Creating a regular schedule for these tasks helps you stay organized and prevents home maintenance from feeling overwhelming. Monthly tasks ensure your home runs smoothly, seasonal maintenance prepares you for weather changes, and yearly inspections address long-term care. By following a plan, you can enjoy a safe, comfortable, and well-maintained home for many years to come.

Protecting Your Investment

Buying a home is one of the biggest financial decisions you'll make, and protecting your investment is just as important as buying it. To keep your property and belongings safe, you'll need to take steps like getting the right insurance, understanding warranties, and using other safety measures. These safeguards ensure your home stays secure, and your money is well-protected.

Homeowner's Insurance

Homeowner's insurance is a must-have for protecting your property. It helps cover the costs of damage caused by events like fires, storms, or theft. For example, if a storm damages your roof or someone breaks into your home and steals your belongings, your insurance will help pay for the repairs or replacements.

When choosing a policy, check what it covers and what it doesn't. Most policies include coverage for the structure of your home, your personal belongings, and liability protection in case someone gets hurt on your property. However, not all events are covered. For instance, you may need extra insurance for floods or earthquakes if you live in areas prone to these risks. Review your policy every year to make sure it still fits your needs.

Home Warranties

A home warranty is different from homeowner's insurance. While insurance covers major damage caused by external events, a warranty focuses on protecting the systems and appliances inside your home. This includes things like your plumbing, heating, air conditioning, and kitchen appliances.

For example, if your refrigerator suddenly stops working or your water heater breaks down, a home warranty can help cover the cost of repairs or replacements. Most warranties charge a small fee each time you make a claim, but they can save you from spending large amounts out of pocket. Make sure to read the warranty details carefully to know what's covered and if there are any limits.

Protecting Your Belongings

Your personal belongings, like furniture, electronics, and clothing, are also part of your investment. Personal property insurance, which is often included in homeowner's policies, helps replace these items if they're stolen or damaged.

To make the process easier, create an inventory of your belongings. Write down a list of everything you own and take photos or videos for proof. If you have valuable items like jewellery or art, you may need extra coverage. Ask your insurance company if they offer special policies for high-value items.

Preventive Measures

Prevention is an important way to protect your property. For example, installing a security system can deter burglars and make your home safer.

Many security systems include cameras, alarms, and motion sensors that alert you and the authorities if there's a problem.

Adding strong locks to doors and windows also improves safety. Outdoor lighting, especially motion-activated lights, can discourage intruders from approaching your home. Some insurance companies even offer discounts if you have a security system, helping you save money while staying safe.

Regular Maintenance

Maintaining your home is just as important as protecting it with insurance and warranties. Regular checks and small fixes can prevent big problems later. For example, inspect your roof for leaks, clean gutters to avoid water damage, and check pipes for any signs of leaks.

Appliances and systems like your HVAC should also be serviced regularly to keep them running efficiently. Fixing small issues early saves money and ensures your home stays in good condition.

Emergency Preparedness

Natural disasters like floods, hurricanes, or wildfires can cause major damage to your home. Preparing for these events can help reduce the risks. Keep an emergency kit with essentials like flashlights, batteries, water, and a first-aid kit.

Learn how to shut off your home's gas, water, and electricity in case of an emergency. If you live in an area prone to hurricanes or earthquakes, consider adding protective features like storm shutters or reinforced roofs.

14

Building Wealth Through Homeownership

Equity and Appreciation

Homeownership is more than just having a place to live. It's a powerful way to build wealth over time. Two important ways this happens are through equity and appreciation. These terms might sound complicated, but they're actually quite simple. Let's break down what they mean and how they help you grow wealth over the years.

What Is Equity?

Equity is the value of your home that you own outright. It's the difference between what your home is worth and how much you owe on your mortgage. For example, if your home is worth $200,000 and you owe $150,000, your equity is $50,000.

Every time you make a mortgage payment, a portion goes toward reducing your loan balance. This increases your equity. Over time, as you pay off more of your mortgage, your equity grows. Eventually, when your home is fully paid off, all of its value becomes your equity.

How to Build Equity Faster

Building equity is like saving money in a bank account, but instead of cash, it's tied to the value of your home. Here are some ways to grow your equity faster:

1. Make Extra Mortgage Payments: Paying more than your required monthly amount reduces your loan balance faster, which increases your equity. Even small extra payments can make a big difference over time.

2. Choose a Shorter Loan Term: A 15-year mortgage allows you to pay off your loan quicker than a 30-year mortgage. While the monthly payments are higher, you'll build equity much faster.
3. Avoid Refinancing Often: Refinancing can extend your loan term, slowing down how quickly you build equity. Refinance only if it saves you money in the long run.

The more equity you have, the more financial options you'll have in the future, like borrowing against it or selling your home for a profit.

What Is Appreciation?

Appreciation is when your home's value increases over time. Many factors can cause a home to appreciate, such as improvements you make, demand for housing in your area, or general market conditions.

For example, if you buy a home for $200,000 and its value increases to $250,000 after five years, your home has appreciated by $50,000. This means your investment has grown without you having to do much at all.

Factors That Influence Appreciation

While appreciation often happens naturally, certain factors can make it happen faster:

1. Location: Homes in desirable areas, like those near good schools, parks, or job opportunities, tend to appreciate more quickly.
2. Home Improvements: Renovations like updating a kitchen, adding energy-efficient windows, or improving curb appeal can increase your home's value.
3. Market Trends: The overall housing market affects appreciation. When demand for homes is high and supply is low, property values often rise.

While you can't control the market, you can make strategic decisions about where you buy and how you improve your home to boost appreciation.

How Equity and Appreciation Work Together

Equity and appreciation work hand-in-hand to grow your wealth. As your home appreciates, the amount of equity you have increases even if you haven't paid off much of your mortgage. For example, if your home value rises from $200,000 to $250,000, your equity grows by $50,000—even if your loan balance hasn't changed.

When you combine regular mortgage payments with natural appreciation, your wealth can grow significantly over time. This is why homeownership is often seen as a smart long-term investment.

Using Equity to Build More Wealth

Once you've built enough equity, you can use it to achieve other financial goals. Here are a few ways to tap into your equity:

1. Home Equity Loan: This lets you borrow against your equity for things like home improvements, education, or starting a business.
2. Home Equity Line of Credit (HELOC): A HELOC works like a credit card, giving you access to funds as needed, based on your equity.
3. Sell Your Home: When you sell your home, the equity becomes cash that you can use for a new home, investments, or other expenses.

Using your equity wisely can help you grow your wealth even further.

The Power of Long-Term Ownership

One of the biggest benefits of owning a home is that both equity and appreciation grow more over time. The longer you own your home, the more wealth you build. For example, in the early years of a mortgage, most of your payments go toward interest. Over time, as your loan balance decreases, more of your payment goes toward building equity. At the same time, appreciation continues to increase the value of your home, multiplying your investment.

Avoiding Risks

While homeownership is a great way to build wealth, it's important to avoid risks that can reduce your equity or appreciation. For example, taking on too much debt against your home's equity can leave you vulnerable if the market changes. Similarly, neglecting maintenance can reduce your home's value over time. Protect your investment by keeping up with repairs and making thoughtful financial decisions.

Using Your Home for Financial Goals

Owning a home is not just about having a place to live—it's also a way to achieve your financial goals. Your home can help you in many ways, like refinancing your mortgage to save money, using a home equity loan to fund important expenses, or earning rental income. Here's how you can make the most of your home to improve your financial future.

Refinancing Your Mortgage

Refinancing is when you replace your current mortgage with a new one that has better terms. This can save you money or help you manage your finances more easily. People often refinance to get a lower interest rate, shorten the loan term, or reduce monthly payments.

For example, if interest rates have dropped since you first got your mortgage, refinancing could lower your monthly payments or reduce the total interest you pay over the life of the loan. Alternatively, if you're earning more now, you could refinance to a shorter loan term—like switching from a 30-year loan to a 15-year loan. This means higher monthly payments, but you'll pay off your home faster and save on interest.

Before refinancing, it's important to check the fees involved, like closing costs, and ensure the savings outweigh these costs. Refinancing can be a great tool if you use it wisely and consider your long-term goals.

Home Equity Loans and Lines of Credit

As you pay down your mortgage and your home's value increases, you build equity. Equity is the difference between what your home is worth and what you still owe. You can use this equity to borrow money for important expenses through a home equity loan or a home equity line of credit (HELOC).

A home equity loan gives you a lump sum of money that you repay over time with fixed monthly payments. This is a good option for one-time expenses like major home repairs, medical bills, or paying for college tuition. For example, if your home is worth $300,000 and you owe $200,000, you may be able to borrow up to $50,000 or more, depending on your lender's rules.

A HELOC, on the other hand, works like a credit card. You can borrow money as needed, up to a set limit, and pay interest only on the amount you use. This option is better for ongoing expenses or projects where you're unsure of the total cost, like a series of home improvements.

Both options use your home as collateral, meaning you risk losing your home if you can't repay the loan. It's important to borrow responsibly and only for things that truly improve your financial situation or quality of life.

Earning Rental Income

Another way to use your home for financial goals is by earning rental income. This can be done by renting out part of your home, like a basement or extra bedroom, or by renting out the entire property if you have another place to live.

For instance, if you have a spare room, you can list it on platforms like Airbnb or rent it to a long-term tenant. This extra income can help cover your mortgage payments, property taxes, or other expenses.

If you decide to rent out your home, there are a few things to consider. First, make sure you understand local laws and regulations about renting.

Some areas have rules about short-term rentals or require you to have a permit. Second, be prepared for additional responsibilities like maintaining the rental space, handling tenant concerns, and paying income taxes on the money you earn. While it takes some effort, renting can provide a steady source of income that helps you reach your financial goals.

Cash-Out Refinancing

Cash-out refinancing is another way to access your home's equity. This option involves replacing your current mortgage with a larger loan and taking the difference in cash. For example, if you owe $150,000 on your mortgage and your home is worth $300,000, you could refinance for $200,000 and use the extra $50,000 for other purposes.

This can be a good choice for large expenses like home renovations, starting a business, or paying off high-interest debt. However, it's important to remember that increasing your mortgage balance means higher monthly payments. You'll also pay interest on the cash-out amount, so use this option carefully.

Downsizing to Save Money

If your current home is larger or more expensive than you need, downsizing can free up money for other financial goals. Selling your home and buying a smaller, less costly property can reduce your monthly expenses and give you extra cash from the sale.

For example, if your home is worth $400,000 and you buy a smaller one for $250,000, the difference can go toward savings, investments, or paying off debt. Downsizing is especially helpful if you're nearing retirement or looking to simplify your lifestyle.

Turning Your Home into an Investment Property

If you decide to move to a new home, you can keep your current property and rent it out as an investment. Owning a rental property can provide a steady income stream and help build long-term wealth as the property value appreciates.

However, becoming a landlord comes with responsibilities, such as finding tenants, handling repairs, and managing finances. Make sure you're prepared for these challenges before turning your home into an investment property.

Planning for Future Upgrades

Upgrading your home is an excellent way to make it more comfortable, functional, and valuable. Smart renovations not only improve your living space but can also increase your home's resale value. Planning upgrades carefully ensures that you get the most out of your investment. Here's how you can choose the right improvements and maximize your home's value.

Start with a Plan

Before making any changes, take the time to plan your upgrades. Think about what improvements your home needs and how they fit into your budget. Prioritize renovations that add value or solve practical issues, like outdated appliances, energy inefficiency, or worn-out spaces.

You can begin by evaluating your home and asking questions like:

- Does the kitchen or bathroom feel outdated?
- Are there areas that need repairs, such as the roof or flooring?
- Would adding space, like a new room or patio, improve the home's usability?

By focusing on what's most important, you can avoid overspending on unnecessary upgrades.

Kitchen Upgrades

The kitchen is often called the heart of the home, and it's one of the first areas buyers notice. Upgrading your kitchen can significantly boost your home's value.

Simple changes like replacing old countertops with granite or quartz, updating cabinet doors, or installing modern fixtures can make the kitchen look fresh and inviting. Adding energy-efficient appliances not only saves money on utility bills but also appeals to eco-conscious buyers. Even small improvements, like a fresh coat of paint or new lighting, can make a big difference.

Bathroom Renovations

Bathrooms are another important area where upgrades can pay off. Buyers value clean, modern bathrooms with updated features. You don't have to spend a fortune to make improvements. Simple updates like replacing old faucets, adding new tiles, or installing a stylish vanity can transform the space.

If you're ready for a bigger project, consider adding a second bathroom or upgrading a half-bath to a full bath. Homes with more bathrooms tend to sell for higher prices because they are more convenient for families.

Energy-Efficient Improvements

Making your home more energy-efficient is a smart way to add value. Today's buyers appreciate homes that are environmentally friendly and cost-effective. Some energy-saving upgrades include:

- Installing solar panels.
- Replacing old windows with energy-efficient models.
- Adding better insulation to keep heating and cooling costs low.

These changes not only increase your home's appeal but also help you save money while you live there.

Outdoor Spaces

Creating usable outdoor spaces is another way to increase your home's value. A well-designed patio, deck, or garden can make your home more attractive to buyers and give you extra space to enjoy.

For example, you could add a wooden deck for entertaining guests or create a landscaped garden for relaxing. Outdoor lighting can also enhance the space and add security. If you already have a yard, regular maintenance like trimming trees and adding fresh plants can boost your home's curb appeal.

Adding More Living Space

If your home feels small, adding extra living space can make it more functional and valuable. Popular options include finishing a basement, converting an attic, or building a home office. These upgrades provide more usable square footage, which can significantly increase your home's resale price.

For example, finishing a basement to create a family room or guest suite makes the space more practical. Adding a home office is particularly appealing now, as more people work from home and need dedicated spaces for productivity.

Updating the Home's Exterior

The outside of your home is the first thing people see, so improving its appearance can make a big impression. Simple upgrades like repainting the exterior, replacing the front door, or adding new siding can make your home look more inviting.

If you have a driveway or walkway, keeping them clean and in good condition also adds to the home's curb appeal. Buyers are often willing to pay more for a house that looks well-maintained from the outside.

Smart Technology

Adding smart home features is becoming increasingly popular. These upgrades make your home more modern and convenient. Examples include:

- Smart thermostats that adjust temperature automatically.
- Smart locks for added security.
- Smart lighting systems that can be controlled with a phone.

These features are especially appealing to tech-savvy buyers and can set your home apart from others on the market.

Avoid Over-Improving

While upgrades can add value, it's important not to over-improve your home. Spending too much on renovations that don't match the overall value of the neighborhood may not give you a good return on investment. For example, installing luxury features in a home located in a modest area may not attract buyers willing to pay extra for those upgrades.

To avoid this, research home prices in your area and focus on improvements that align with what buyers expect.

Work with Professionals

Some upgrades are best left to professionals, especially if they involve structural changes, plumbing, or electrical work. Hiring skilled contractors ensures the job is done correctly and safely. Before starting any major renovation, get multiple quotes, check references, and make sure the contractor is licensed and insured.

Building a Legacy Through Real Estate

Homeownership is more than just a personal achievement; it's a way to create lasting benefits for your family and community. When you own a home, you're building a foundation that can support your loved ones for years and even generations. It's not just about having a place to live—it's about creating stability, financial security, and opportunities for those who come after you. Let's explore how homeownership can help you leave a meaningful legacy.

Generational Wealth for Your Family

Owning a home is one of the best ways to build wealth that can be passed down to your children and grandchildren. Over time, as you pay off your mortgage and your property value increase, your home becomes an asset with significant value. This is known as equity—the part of your home that you own outright.

When you leave your home to your family, they inherit this equity. For example, if your home is worth $300,000 and you've paid off your mortgage, your family can sell the home or use it as a source of financial stability. This inheritance can help them pay for college, start a business, or even buy their own homes, giving them opportunities, they might not have had otherwise.

Stability for Future Generations

Owning a home provides a stable environment for your family. When you have a permanent place to live, your children can grow up in the same neighborhood, attend the same schools, and build lasting friendships. This sense of stability is important for emotional well-being and helps create a strong sense of community.

For future generations, this stability can continue. If your children inherit your home, they won't have to worry about finding a place to live or dealing with rising rent prices. A home that stays in the family offers a sense of security and continuity, giving your loved ones a place, they can always call their own.

Encouraging Financial Responsibility

When you own a home, you're not just investing in property—you're also teaching valuable lessons about financial responsibility. Paying a mortgage, budgeting for maintenance, and managing property taxes show your family the importance of long-term planning and money management.

These lessons can be passed down to your children. When they see you making smart financial decisions and working to maintain your home, they'll be more likely to develop good habits themselves. This knowledge prepares them to take on the responsibility of owning their own homes someday, continuing the cycle of financial growth and stability.

Strengthening the Community

Homeownership doesn't just benefit your family; it also strengthens the community. When you own a home, you're more likely to stay in the area for a long time, which helps build connections with your neighbours. Strong neighbourhoods with stable homeowners create a sense of pride and belonging that benefits everyone.

As a homeowner, you contribute to the local economy by paying property taxes. These taxes fund public services like schools, parks, and road maintenance, making the community a better place for everyone. By maintaining your property and being an active member of the neighborhood, you set an example that encourages others to do the same.

Creating Opportunities for Others

A home can also be used to create opportunities for others. For example, if you have extra space, you can rent it out to someone who needs housing. This not only provides income for you but also helps others find a safe and affordable place to live.

In the future, your home could also be used as a resource for family members who need a temporary place to stay. Whether it's a relative going through a tough time or a young adult saving for their own home, having a family-owned property offers support and flexibility.

Passing Down Memories

A home is more than just a building; it's a place where memories are made. The holidays, birthdays, and everyday moments spent with loved ones turn a house into a special place that holds emotional value.

When you pass your home down to your family, you're not just giving them a financial asset—you're giving them a place filled with memories and a sense of belonging. This emotional connection makes the home even more valuable and strengthens family bonds.

Inspiring the Next Generation

When your family sees the impact of homeownership, it can inspire them to achieve the same goals. Children who grow up in a home owned by their parents are more likely to become homeowners themselves. They understand the benefits of owning property and work toward creating their own legacy.

By sharing your experiences and showing how homeownership has helped your family, you can motivate the next generation to build their own wealth through real estate. This creates a ripple effect, where each generation builds on the success of the one before it.

Protecting Your Legacy

To ensure your home continues to benefit your family, it's important to protect your legacy. This means keeping your home in good condition through regular maintenance and making sure it's properly insured. You should also create a plan for passing the property down, such as writing a will or setting up a trust.

Clear communication with your family about your intentions helps avoid confusion or disagreements later. When everyone understands the value and purpose of the home, they're more likely to work together to preserve it for future generations.

Conclusion

Owning your own home is a remarkable achievement, and it's important to take a moment to reflect on all the effort and determination it took to get here. Buying a home is not just about signing papers or moving boxes—it's about months, maybe even years, of planning, saving, and making smart decisions. Every choice you made, every sacrifice, and every bit of patience has led you to this point. It wasn't always easy, but your resilience and focus brought you through. This is a milestone worth celebrating, so take pride in what you have accomplished.

Your new home represents more than just a place to live. It stands as a symbol of your hard work, independence, and strength. For Black women, especially, homeownership holds a unique power. It challenges the barriers that have stood for generations and shows what is possible when determination meets opportunity. Your success paves the way for others, offering hope and proof that this dream can be achieved. Each small step you took—from saving for a down payment to learning about mortgages—has added up to something truly life-changing.

For those who are just starting this journey or feel unsure if they can do it, let your experience be a source of encouragement. Homeownership is not just for other people—it is for you, too. There will be obstacles, and there will be moments when it feels overwhelming, but it's important to remember that every step brings you closer to something amazing. For other Black women who may face unique challenges, know that you have the strength to overcome them. Support systems, education, and determination can help you achieve your dreams. Sharing your story and knowledge with others can inspire them to take the first steps toward owning their own homes.

Now that you're a homeowner, your journey isn't over—it has simply changed. Maintaining your home is key to keeping it a source of pride and security.

Treating your home with care and attention will not only preserve its value but also make it a place you love coming back to every day. Regular upkeep, from cleaning gutters to fixing small repairs before they grow into big problems, is an important part of homeownership. These tasks may seem like a chore at first, but they are investments in your future. They ensure that your home remains a safe, comfortable, and beautiful space for years to come.

Homeownership is also about the emotional connection you create with your space. Take the time to make your house feel truly like your home. Fill it with things that bring you joy, whether that's family photos, cozy furniture, or colourful walls that reflect your personality. This is your sanctuary, a place where you can recharge and build memories. Your relationship with your home will grow over time, and taking care of it will feel less like work and more like an act of love and respect for what you've built.

As you settle into your new lifestyle, it's also a good time to think about what comes next. Homeownership opens doors to new opportunities, whether that's improving your financial situation, building wealth, or helping others achieve their goals. You might consider investing in a second property, whether as a rental or for future growth. You could explore home improvements that add value and make your space even more enjoyable. Or, you might simply focus on enjoying the life you've worked so hard to create. Whatever your next steps, the skills and discipline you've gained during this process will help guide you toward even greater achievements.

Owning a home can also allow you to give back to your community. By becoming a part of your neighborhood, you contribute to its strength and vibrancy. Your presence and actions make a difference, whether it's helping a neighbour, supporting local businesses, or simply being a positive role model. Homeownership is not just about personal success—it's about building a foundation that uplifts others as well.

Sharing your knowledge and encouraging others to achieve their dreams can have a ripple effect, inspiring more Black women to pursue homeownership and all the opportunities it offers.

While it's important to think about the future, it's equally important to enjoy the present. Take time to appreciate what you've accomplished. Sit in your favourite corner of your new home, enjoy the space you've created, and remind yourself of how far you've come. Homeownership is not just a goal—it's a lifestyle that offers freedom, security, and joy. Every small improvement you make, every quiet evening you spend in your home, and every celebration with family and friends will add to the value of this accomplishment.

Looking ahead, remember that homeownership is a journey that continues to grow with you. Your home will evolve as your life does, adapting to new needs and goals. Whether you're building wealth, creating a legacy for your family, or simply living your best life, your home is a powerful tool to help you achieve those dreams.

Treat it with care, share your experience with others, and continue to build on this incredible achievement. You've earned this moment, and the future is full of possibilities. Celebrate it fully, and look forward to all the wonderful things that lie ahead.

Made in the USA
Monee, IL
04 November 2026

67381353R10108